GOSPEL TRUTH

Adam Curtis

ivp

GOSPEL TRUTH

Answering
New Atheist attacks
on the Gospels

Paul Barnett

Inter-Varsity Press
Norton Street, Nottingham NG7 3HR, England
Email: ivp@ivpbooks.com
Website: www.ivpbooks.com

First published 2012

British Library Cataloguing in Publication Data
A catalogue record for this book is available from the British Library.

ISBN: 978–1–84474–594–4

Set in Monotype Garamond 11/14pt
Typeset in Great Britain by CRB Associates, Potterhanworth, Lincolnshire
Printed and bound in Great Britain by Ashford Colour Press Ltd, Gosport,
Hampshire

*Inter-Varsity Press publishes Christian books that are true to the Bible and that communicate
the gospel, develop discipleship and strengthen the church for its mission in the world.*

*Inter-Varsity Press is closely linked with the Universities and Colleges Christian Fellowship,
a student movement connecting Christian Unions in universities and colleges throughout Great
Britain, and a member movement of the International Fellowship of Evangelical Students.
Website: www.uccf.org.uk.*

CONTENTS

FIGURES AND TABLES

Figures

Tables

PREFACE

Like most people I have been aware of the rise of aggressive atheism in recent years. The proactive atheism of some leading academics has been channelled at a popular level against the teaching of various faiths in schools and in protests against historical religious festivals. Atheism threatens the religious basis of law and culture in societies for which religion – Christianity in particular – has played such an important part. The atheists' objective seems to be the eradication of religion from the public square and its replacement by a comprehensive 'politically correct' secularism.

Radical atheism understands the importance of the Bible, the New Testament in particular, for the survival of Christianity. Destroy the credibility of the gospel story and you destroy the credibility of Jesus and, thereby, the credibility of God.

This book takes note of some of the atheists' attacks on the historical basis of Christianity, which it seeks to answer. It is important for me to declare that I am a committed Christian and church minister, now retired. I am, however, also a practising historian who seeks to address historical issues as objectively as possible, whilst recognizing that absolute objectivity is not possible for anyone.

My approach in general is to point to the 'big picture' evidence for the rise of Christianity and to discuss individual issues – and there are some – from the overall perspective of the first century or so of Christianity. It is my conviction, based on sound evidence, that the case for the integrity of the New Testament is intellectually compelling. Equally, I am convinced that an honest person can accept the probity of these documents in good conscience, as distinct from a faith commitment.

Some of the underlying research material in this book was provided by a junior colleague, Robert Martin, which I acknowledge with grateful thanks.

ABBREVIATIONS

1 Apol.	*First Apology* (Justin Martyr)
ABD	*Anchor Bible Dictionary*, ed. D. N. Freedman, 6 vols. (New York: Doubleday, 1992)
AD	Anno Domini (after Christ)
Ann.	*Annals of Imperial Rome* (Tacitus)
Ant.	*Jewish Antiquities* (Josephus)
AUC	*Ab urbe condita* (*From the Founding of the City*) (Livy)
Aug.	*Divus Augustus* (*The Divine Augustus*) (Suetonius)
b. Ber.	*Babylonian Talmud Berakot*
b. Meṣ.	*Babylonian Talmud Meṣiʿa*
b. Sanh.	*Babylonian Talmud Sanhedrin*
BBR	*Bulletin for Biblical Research*
BC	before Christ
Bib	*Biblica*
bk.	book
C.	century
c.	*circa*
Claud.	*Divus Claudius* (*The Divine Claudius*) (Suetonius)
Clem.	Clement (of Rome)
d.	died
Dial.	*Dialogue with Trypho* (Justin Martyr)

Eph.	*Ephesians* (Ignatius)
ESV	English Standard Version
ET	English Translation
Eum.	*Eumenides* (Aeschylus)
ExpTim	*Expository Times*
Flacc.	*In Flaccum (Against Flaccus)* (Philo)
Geogr.	*Geography* (Strabo)
Gk.	Greek
Haer.	*Adversus haereses (Against Heresies)* (Irenaeus)
Hist.	*Histories* (Tacitus)
Hist. eccl.	*Historia ecclesiastica (Church History)* (Eusebius)
Hist. Rom.	*Historia Romana (Roman History)* (Dio Cassius)
History	*History of Rome* (Livy)
HTR	*Harvard Theological Review*
Hypoth.	*Hypothetica* (Philo)
IG	*Inscriptiones graecae*
Inf. Gosp. Thom.	*The Infancy Gospel of Thomas*
JETS	*Journal of the Evangelical Theological Society*
JR	*Journal of Religion*
JSNTSup	Journal for the Study of the New Testament, Supplement Series
LCL	Loeb Classical Library
Legat.	*Legatio ad Gaium (On the Embassy to Gaius)* (Philo)
m. Nid.	*Mishna Niddah*
m. Roš Haš.	*Mishna Roš Haššanah*
m. Suk.	*Mishna Sukkah*
m. Ta'an.	*Mishna Ta'anit*
Nat.	*Natural History* (Pliny the Elder)
NCB	New Century Bible
NICNT	New International Commentary on the New Testament
NIGTC	New International Greek Testament Commentary
NovT	*Novum Testamentum*
NTS	*New Testament Studies*

OT	Old Testament
P	papyrus
Philadelph.	*Philadelphians* (Ignatius)
Phil.	*Philippians* (Polycarp)
Prob.	*Quod omnis probus liber sit* (*That Every Good Person Is Free*) (Philo)
Res gest. divi Aug.	*Res gestae divi Augusti* (*Deeds of the Divine Augustus*) (Augustus Caesar)
Rom.	*Romans* (Ignatius)
RTR	*Reformed Theological Review*
Smyrn.	*Smyrnaeans* (Ignatius)
Spect.	*De spectaculis* (*The Shows*) (Tertullian)
Strom.	*Stromata* (*Miscellanies*) (Clement of Alexandria)
tr.	translated by, translation
Trall.	*Trallians* (Ignatius)
VC	*Vigiliae christianae*
War	*Jewish War* (Josephus)

1. INTRODUCTION: NEW ATHEISM AND GOSPEL TRUTH

If I give you a rose, you will not disdain its creator.

Tertullian

Philosophers debate whether to define atheism in negative terms, as a lack of belief in God, or positively as the declared disbelief in God. The derivation of the word 'atheist' does not help us since the two Greek words *a* (without) and *theos* (God) mean only 'godless'. For the purpose of this book atheism is understood in the positive sense, as the asserted disbelief in God.

At the popular level atheists based their disbelief on the invisibility of God. A schoolboy said to a friend, 'Show me a photograph of God and I will believe,' and an acquaintance said to me, 'I will believe only what I can see, smell, hear or touch.'

Beyond that, however, atheists point to the evils in the world that deny the existence of a God who is both all-powerful and good. Besides, they say, many of these evils were caused by religious wars.

There is nothing new about atheism. The ancient Epicureans were 'atheists'.

Epicurus (341–270 BC) dismissed the idea of God or the gods and directed all his attention to the material world, on things that can be seen and touched. Ironically the Romans, who worshipped hand-made gods, called the early Christians 'atheists' because they did not believe in gods that could be seen.

Since the Enlightenment there have been prominent atheists, for example Bertrand Russell and George Bernard Shaw. Communist Russia of the twentieth century was avowedly and determinedly atheistic.

The first years of the third millennium saw the rise of those who called themselves 'new' atheists. 'Old' atheists were content to mock and ridicule believers, but the 'new' atheists aggressively seek to drive them out of the public square. Its militancy distinguished it as 'new'. The unifying concept of the New Atheists is their decision that 'the traditional atheist policy of diplomatic reticence [towards religion] should be discarded'.[1]

The main protagonists of this anti-religious movement are the self-styled 'four horsemen': Richard Dawkins, Sam Harris, Daniel Dennett and Christopher Hitchens.[2] There are other New Atheist writers,[3] but it is primarily the 'four horsemen' who have captured public attention and are visibly identified as the leaders of this movement.[4]

---

1. S. Hooper, 'The Rise of the "New Atheists"', *CNN.com*, accessed 7 July 2009.

2. The original 'four horsemen' were Richard Dawkins, Sam Harris, Daniel Dennett and Carl Sagan. Sagan died in 1986 and Christopher Hitchens, who took his place, died in 2011.

3. Such as M. Onfray, *The Atheist Manifesto: The Case Against Christianity, Judaism and Islam* (ET Melbourne: Melbourne University Press, 2005).

4. R. Dawkins, *The God Delusion* (London: Bantam, 2006); D. C. Dennett, *Breaking the Spell: Religion as a Natural Phenomenon* (London: Allen Lane, 2006); S. Harris, *The End of Faith: Religion, Terror and the Future of Reason* (New York: Norton, 2004); C. Hitchens, *God Is Not Great: How Religion Poisons Everything* (New York: Twelve, 2007).

Rise of 'New' Atheism

How can we explain the sudden rise of 'New' Atheism? The views of leaders such as Richard Dawkins are not new, but they seem to have developed their momentum during the first decade of the new millennium. Is this because it was a *new* millennium, a time to instigate radical departures from the old ways of thinking? If so this would indeed be ironical since western calendars date millennia from the birth of Jesus! One related suggestion is the unwelcome and unexpected upsurge of religion – Christian, Islamic, Buddhist – that was evident in the latter decades of the twentieth century. According to Micklethwait and Wooldridge, it was these 'retrograde' revivals of religion that provoked the secular fury of Dawkins and his colleagues to argue that all religion is based on superstition and has no place in science-informed modernity.[5] Christopher Hitchens was typically trenchant:

> Religion has run out of justifications. Thanks to the telescope and the microscope, it no longer offers an explanation of anything important. Where once it used to be able, by its total command of a worldview, to *prevent* the emergence of rivals, it can now only impede and retard – or try to turn back – the measurable advances that we have made.[6]

Or, is this hostility explained by a terrible event at the beginning of the new millennium, an event inspired by religion? On 11 September 2001 a small number of convinced Muslim believers launched devastating attacks upon buildings and people in the United States, the reverberations of which will continue for decades.

Whatever the catalyst was that inspired the crusade of the 'New' Atheists, their credo is that all religion is evil and a danger to be driven from society.

---

5. J. Micklethwait and A. Wooldridge, *God Is Back* (New York: Penguin, 2009), pp. 15–16, 21.

6. Hitchens, *God Is Not Great*, p. 282, italics original.

Influence of 'New' Atheism

In addition to their prolific writings, the prominent 'new' atheists have criss-crossed traditionally Christian countries giving lectures and setting up debates with church leaders, frequently before large audiences. Formerly sleepy rationalist societies, whose members now flood the correspondence columns of daily newspapers at every opportunity, have been emboldened and empowered. Their members lobby politicians to dispense with religious teaching in public schools and for the removal of Christian festivals such as Christmas and Easter from the public calendars. The academic atheists have influential friends within the media who take pleasure in expanding on every mistake by prominent Christians. At their inspiration there is a sustained attempt to secularize Judeo-Christian societies. Christians in particular are a soft target, for non-retaliation is a fundamental teaching of Jesus.

Their strategy

In brief the 'New' Atheists use three main arguments against religion – philosophical, scientific and biblical (yes, biblical). These arguments are, in effect, arguments against Christianity; other religions do not get the same attention. Philosophical and moral issues are fully dealt with elsewhere,[7] but I will make brief reference to the scientific issues here, before devoting the remainder of this book to the biblical concerns.

Let me admit immediately that I am a layman in the realm of science. Nonetheless, there are – as there have always been – many

---

7. Francis Collins struggled with many such issues in the course of his journey as a Christian: see F. Collins, *The Language of God* (New York: Free Press, 2006), pp. 33–54. See also e.g. J. Lennox, *Gunning for God* (Oxford: Lion, 2011); D. Glass, *Atheism's New Clothes* (Nottingham: Apollos, 2012).

highly accomplished scientists who are convinced Christians whose views are worth hearing.

Scientists who are Christian

In 1978 Professor Graeme Clark rewrote the rules of hearing by inventing and implanting the world's first bionic ear. Clark is now exploring the same understanding of electric stimulation of nerves for helping paraplegics, even for the development of the bionic eye.

In 2007 Clark delivered the *Boyer Lectures* for the Australian Broadcasting Commission.[8] He observed that there are

> 100 thousand million nerve cells in the adult human brain, roughly the same number as the number of stars in the Milky Way. Each brain cell is connected to between 10 and 10,000 other brain cells, so that there are 100 million million connections in the brain. So there are an amazing number of possibilities in the brain for sensing and processing information. Our conscious experiences depend not only on the vast network of brain cells and connections but also on their interaction with the complex chemistry of the cell.

Clark asks:

> could the physical universe, which physicists now show had only the remotest chance of producing carbon-based life, have evolved into human consciousness by mindless chance? I think not. The human brain is so sophisticated a mechanism that scientists have still not been able to design engineering systems that can match its crucial functions. For me that means a supernatural entity, namely God, was responsible, rather than saying it assembled itself by mindless chance. In any case, a human being would have to know everything to know there is no God!

---

8. *Restoring the Senses*, Lecture 1, Boyer Lectures, Australian Broadcasting Commission, 1978.

Clark refers also to

> vision as another remarkable sense. More than a million nerve fibers are
> needed for the visual pathways to represent a scene. . . . The spinal cord
> also is very complex. At all levels the sensory and motor stimuli interact,
> and can influence each other, often without your knowing it or being able
> to control it. For example, when you step forward with say your left leg,
> the muscles in the right leg are kept rigid, so that you don't overbalance.

Clark points to the thumb as

> an outstanding example of the integration of the senses. To give it such
> fine control, its muscles have more receptors than other muscles in the
> body. The thumb is so unique that two sculptors in communist and
> atheistic Russia were in such awe that they set up an altar and worshipped
> the god of the thumb.

Originally an agnostic, Francis Collins progressed to atheism
during his PhD studies in physical chemistry at Yale. En route,
however, he also broadened his interests to biochemistry and became
seized by the principles of DNA and protein. Collins then transferred
to medical studies, during the course of which he was confronted by
the quiet faith of an older woman who was dying and who asked
Collins about what he believed. This began a process of enquiry that
reached a climax in his conversion to Christianity.[9]

> I had started this journey of intellectual exploration to confirm my
> atheism. That now lay in ruins as the argument from the moral law
> (and many other issues) forced me to admit the plausibility of the God
> hypothesis. Agnosticism, which had seemed like a safe second-place
> haven, now loomed like the great cop-out it often is. Faith in God now
> seemed more rational than unbelief.[10]

---

9. Collins, *Language of God*, pp. 20–21.
10. Ibid., p. 30.

Francis Collins went on professionally to become the head of the prestigious Human Genome Project. By any measure, Collins is one of the world's leading scientists.

Another eminent scientist, John Lennox, Professor of Mathematics at Oxford University, also addresses the arguments of the New Atheists.[11] Lennox systematically engages with the issues in cosmology, biology, the origins of life and genetics. He cites the arguments of sceptics and sets out scientific reasons for an Intelligent Mind as the source of the universe and of life. He summarizes his conclusions as follows:

> although science with all its power cannot address some of the fundamental questions that we ask, nevertheless the universe contains certain clues as to our relationship to it, clues that are scientifically accessible. The rational intelligibility of the universe, for instance, points to the existence of a Mind that was responsible both for the universe and our minds. It is for this reason that we are able to do science and to discover the beautiful mathematical structures that underlie the phenomena we can observe. Not only that, but our increasing insight into the fine tuning of the universe in general, and of the planet earth in particular, is consistent with the widespread awareness that we are meant to be here. The earth is our home.[12]

Scientific studies, however, have their limitations in relationship with God. Lennox quotes many prominent physicists, cosmologists, biologists and geneticists, some of them Nobel Prize winners, who affirm the existence of the Mind who is the source of the material universe and the human mind. Nonetheless, we depend upon the Bible for the 'revelation' of the identity of that Intelligent Mind, his character and his manner of relationships with the created order, including with us humans. This makes the Bible uniquely and

---

11. J. Lennox, *God's Undertaker: Has Science Buried God?* (Oxford: Lion, 2009).

12. Ibid., p. 207.

indispensably important in the quest for truth and meaning, a subject to which we will return at the conclusion of this chapter.[13]

Atheists and gospel truth

Crusading atheists who seek to disprove God make historical attacks on the Gospels as a major part of their strategy. According to Hitchens, 'The case for biblical consistency or authenticity or "inspiration" has been in tatters for some time, and the rents and tears only become more obvious with better research, and thus no "revelation" can be derived from that quarter.'[14] This book responds to the claims of Hitchens and other sceptics that the Gospels are inconsistent. Their instincts, however, are correct: destroy the credibility of the Gospels and you destroy the credibility of Jesus and thus the credibility of God.

This prompts the question about the competence of the atheists to pass judgment on the Gospels. Dawkins and Hitchens, for example, are leading figures in their respective fields; Dawkins is an eminent evolutionary biologist and Hitchens was a brilliant political commentator. Distinction in these fields of scholarship, however, does not qualify them as authorities in Gospels studies.

Dawkins refers to anecdotes about the boy Jesus in the *Gospel of Thomas* that he confuses with the *Infancy Gospel of Thomas*. In any case, these are apocryphal works written centuries after Jesus.[15] Worse, he attributes the story of the wise men (Magi) to the Gospel of Luke, when it actually appears in the Gospel of Matthew![16] Dawkins also makes the ludicrous claim that the Gospels are as

---

13. Scientists such as Francis Collins are acutely aware of moral and philosophical issues related to their belief in God. See Collins, *Language of God*, pp. 33–54.
14. Hitchens, *God Is Not Great*, p. 122.
15. Dawkins, *God Delusion*, p. 96.
16. Ibid., p. 94.

much works of fiction as Dan Brown's *The Da Vinci Code*.[17] One of the results of painstaking research into ancient biographies and the Gospels has been to reveal that the Gospels belong to the genre of biography, not fiction.[18] All credit to Dawkins for his accomplishment in his chosen area of scholarship, but his basic errors about the Gospels diminish his credibility to pass historical judgments on them.

History, the Gospels and God

These atheists are, indeed, right in their attacks on the historical consistency of the Gospels. To destroy that consistency would mean a serious issue of credibility about Jesus and the God he claimed to represent and reveal. American scholar George Eldon Ladd understood this well:

> The uniqueness and scandal of the Christian religion rests on mediation of revelation through *historical* events . . . And if those facts should be disproved, Christianity would be false. This, however, is what makes Christianity unique because unlike other world religions, modern man has means of actually verifying Christianity's truth by historical evidence.[19]

Accomplished scientists such as Clark, Collins and Lennox are able to point to a deity outside the creation who is the source and origin of creation, and who is infinitely intelligent and powerful. The claim of the Gospels, however, is that in the Son of God, his words and works, we see fully the Father from whom he came. 'No

---

17. Ibid., p. 97.
18. For references to this research see C. S. Keener, 'Otho: A Targeted Comparison of Suetonius' Biography and Tacitus' History, with Implications for the Gospels' Reliability', *BBR* 21.3 (2011), p. 331, nn. 1–2.
19. Quoted in P. Copan (ed.), *Will the Real Jesus Please Stand Up* (Grand Rapids: Baker, 1998), p. 24.

one has ever seen God,' wrote John, 'the only Son, who is at the
Father's side, he has made him known' (John 1:18). Furthermore,
the Son of God not only fully reveals the otherwise imperfectly
known God; he also connects that God to us humans and makes us
his children.

The issue of gospel truth, that is, of the gospel's *historical* truth,
is of critical importance. Destroy that truth and the whole structure
of Christian belief and practice crumbles and collapses. The vindi-
cation of gospel truth, however, demands that we give it our close
attention. It is good to begin with the 'big picture', however, and to
that we now turn.

2. GOSPEL TRUTH AND THE BIG PICTURE

'I am the Alpha and the Omega,' says the Lord God, 'who is and who was and who is to come, the Almighty.'

Revelation 1:8

This book is about the importance of gospel truth, without which it is impossible truly to know God, or, as St Paul more precisely says, to be known *by* God. The conversion of C. S. Lewis to Christianity illustrates this point.

Formerly an aggressive atheist, Lewis had gradually become a theist but was not yet a Christian. In 1926 an unlikely chance encounter with T. R. Weldon, a noted sceptic, proved to be a critical link in Lewis's spiritual journey.[1] Weldon, a fellow academic at Oxford, commented that there was good evidence supporting the historicity of the Gospels, adding, 'Rum thing, that stuff of Frazer's about the Dying God. It almost looks as if it really happened once.'[2]

Weldon, although a sceptic, was implying that the resurrection of Christ may have happened after all and that Sir James Frazer's

---

1. This conversation is reported in G. Sayer, *Jack: A Life of C. S. Lewis* (London: Hodder & Stoughton, 1997), p. 222.
2. Ibid.

popular theories about dying and rising gods in eastern religions during the era of Christ were 'rum stuff'.[3]

This remark prompted Lewis to study the Gospels and, as a result, he pronounced them historically reliable. At about the same time he encountered G. K. Chesterton's paradox about Christ, that he must be either a fraud, or deluded or the Son of God. This paradox arises from apparently contradictory things about Christ, that on one hand he said, 'I am the light of the world,' but on the other said, 'I am meek and humble of heart.' The power of this paradox depends on confidence that the Gospels are historically based. If Lewis had not trusted the veracity of these texts, the dilemma about Christ would have had no power to move him from theism to Christian belief.

The manner of Lewis's conversion focuses our attention on the Gospels and their underlying historical truth.

The New Atheists' attack on gospel truth

If confidence in 'gospel' truth has the power to convert, it is no surprise that crusading atheists believe that denial of that truth has the power to deconvert. It is understandable that New Atheists such as Richard Dawkins attack the historical reliability of the Gospels.

For the moment, let me briefly mention some points of their attack:

- Jesus did not actually exist.
- There are contradictions between the Gospels and world history.
- There are contradictions between the Gospels.
- Miracles are impossible.
- The gospel transmission is unreliable.

---

3. As an atheist Lewis had been influenced by Frazer, who in his famous book *The Golden Bough* (1890) argued that human belief had progressed through three stages: primitive magic, replaced by religion, in turn replaced by science (Sayer, *Jack*, pp. 112–113).

I will discuss these later, but first it will be important for us to stand back and see the first century of Christianity from the wide angle of historical perspective.

Dating the New Testament

Jesus was born in 6 BC and was crucified in AD 33.[4] By about AD 40 the wider population of Antioch in Syria had invented a name for a new sect, calling its members 'Christians' (literally 'followers of Christ'). In AD 110 Ignatius, the church leader of Antioch,[5] referred to this movement as 'Christianity', the first known use of that word.

What, then, did Christianity teach? Ignatius has this to say about Christ in what seems to have been a simple church creed:

> Jesus Christ . . . was of the stock of David, who was from Mary, who was truly born, [ate] and drank, was truly persecuted under Pontius Pilate, was truly crucified and died . . . who also was truly raised from the dead, His Father raising him . . .[6]

Ignatius clearly based these words on the Gospels, without directly quoting them. In fact, Ignatius knows three of the four Gospels since we find echoes of their words scattered throughout his seven

---

4. Jesus was born in the latter years of King Herod, who died in 4 BC. Because John the Baptist began preaching in AD 29 (cf. Luke 3:1–2) it points to AD 33 as the date of Jesus' crucifixion, although many prefer AD 30. For the AD 30 date see R. Riesner, *Paul's Early Period* (Grand Rapids: Eerdmans, 1998), pp. 52–58; and for the AD 33 date see H. Hoehner, *Chronological Aspects of the Life of Christ* (Grand Rapids: Zondervan, 1979), pp. 95–113.

5. Ignatius, Bishop of Antioch, wrote his seven short letters as a prisoner en route to Rome where he knew he faced martyrdom.

6. *Letter to the Trallians* 9.4, quoted in J. N. D. Kelly, *Early Christian Creeds* (London: Longmans, 1963), p. 68.

letters.[7] This leads us to conclude that these Gospels were in circulation before Ignatius wrote his letters (in AD 110).

So when were the four Gospels written? Logically we conclude that they were written between AD 33 (when Jesus was killed) and AD 110 (when Ignatius wrote his letters). Although we do not know the precise dates, most scholars think Mark was written by AD 70 and the other three during the next decade or so.[8] This means our earliest Gospel was written about thirty-five years after Jesus and the others no more than about fifty years after him. Some date the Gospels a few years earlier and some a few years later, but either way this does not alter the fact that each was written within a lifetime of the lifespan of Jesus.

By the standards of those times these were relatively brief 'lead times' separating a biography from its subject. Approximately ninety years elapsed before Suetonius (in AD 130) wrote his 'life' of Tiberius, the Caesar under whom Jesus was crucified. The closeness of time between the Gospels and Jesus is all the more remarkable since he was, relatively, speaking, a nobody, merely a despised Jew, from remote Galilee on the edge of the empire, who had been crucified for treason, and who was said to have been resurrected. It would be difficult to think of a less likely candidate for world rule!

The letters of Paul, written between AD 48 (Galatians) and AD 65 (the year of Paul's death), are even closer to Jesus than the Gospels. Paul wrote to the Galatians in AD 48, to the Thessalonians in 50 and 51, to the Corinthians in 55 and 56, and to the Romans in 57.

We are not able to date the letters of James and Peter but they were probably written within the same span as Paul's letters.

In fact, the letters and Gospels that comprise the New Testament,

---

7. E.g. we find Matt. 12:33 in *Eph.* 14.2, Luke 24:39 in *Smyrn.* 3.2 and John 3:8 in *Philadelph.* 7.1. Both Matthew and Luke incorporate Mark, implying Mark's authorship prior to Matthew and Luke.

8. J. Crossley, *The Date of Mark's Gospel: Insight from the Law in Earliest Christianity*, JSNTSup 266 (London: T. & T. Clark, 2004), argues that the Gospel of Mark was written in the 30s.

twenty-seven documents in total, were written between AD 33 and AD 100 (see fig. 2.1 below).

Fig. 2.1 Timeline: Jesus, Paul's letters and the Gospels.

Mission literature

Educated people in the era of the New Testament were interested in historical writing and biographies. Josephus wrote two massive histories about the Jews as well as his own autobiography, and Tacitus wrote two historical works and a biography. Both authors wrote to inform their readers about past events and people, but in each case with a strong point of view. Josephus wrote the *Jewish War* to warn the Jews not to rebel against the might of Rome, whilst Tacitus' *Annals of Imperial Rome* portrays the Caesars as those who betrayed the ideals of the Roman republic. Nonetheless these writers would have realized the limitations of the circulation of their works since each had to be laboriously copied by scribes.

This explains why so few manuscripts of these important works have survived. There are only nine copies of the *Jewish War* (the oldest of which is from the tenth century) and just one of the *Annals* (which is incomplete and from the fifteenth century).

By contrast, there are many hundreds of manuscripts of New Testament texts, whether as a surviving fragment of a book (P[52], the early second-century fragment of John 18), as a semi-complete individual book (P[75], mid-second-century John), as a collection of the Gospels and the Acts (P[45], a late second-century codex), as a collection of the letters of Paul and Hebrews (P[46], a late second-century codex) or as a complete New Testament (Codex Sinaiticus – from the fourth century).

Furthermore as the Christian message spread further afield its texts were translated from Greek into Latin, Syriac, Coptic and Armenian. This plethora of New Testament texts is indeed striking when one considers the paucity of surviving texts of Josephus and Tacitus.

There is a simple explanation for this. The message about Christ was initially a verbal message. Jesus was a teacher and his original followers were teachers of a message they called 'the gospel' (which meant 'good and important news'). That oral 'message' was centred on Christ, his deeds, teaching, death and resurrection. Once congregations of believers had been established, leaders such as Paul, James, Peter, John, Jude and the author of Hebrews wrote their letters to confirm these churches in the faith. These letters were probably the earliest written form of Christian mission literature, which continued throughout the era of the apostles into the next century in the pastoral letters of Clement, Ignatius and Polycarp to the churches and individuals of their day.

Why, then, did the early Christians need to write the Gospels when they already possessed that message in oral forms and in the letters? The most likely reason was the passing of great leaders such as James, Peter and Paul, who were each killed during the sixties. Their deaths pointed to the need for more permanent records of Jesus. The oral gospel became the written gospel 'according to' four authors, Matthew, Mark, Luke and John.

Why were there *four* Gospels? It was because there were basically four mission groups that had emerged in the first decades after Jesus, led respectively by James, Peter, John and Paul.[9] Each mission group produced pastoral letters for their networks of congregations and each group produced a Gospel – Matthew (for James's mission

9. The four leaders met to devise missionary strategy in Jerusalem in AD 47 (Gal. 2:6–9). In the decades following, letters and Gospels were written for their respective mission networks. See E. E. Ellis, *The Making of the New Testament Documents* (Leiden: Brill, 2002), pp. 307–319.

network), Mark (for Peter's mission network), Luke-Acts (for Paul's mission network) and John (for John's mission network).

Why did this mission literature survive? There is one simple explanation. Each letter and Gospel was written and sent to the mission churches to be *repeatedly* read aloud. As in the synagogues, where only texts recognized as 'holy Scripture' were read aloud, so it was that the public reading of apostolic texts in the churches conveyed upon them the special status of 'Scripture'.

As new churches were established, copies of apostolic writings were needed. In the first decade after Jesus there were churches throughout the land of Israel, within the province of Syria and probably also in Rome. By the second decade we know also of congregations in Asia Minor and Greece, but there were probably churches in other places as well. This was an accelerating process, one where hostile commentators such as Tacitus and Pliny described Christianity as a spreading disease. The persecutions of Christians in the second and third centuries did not halt the rapid growth of Christianity. Once Constantine made Christianity the state religion, the need for more scriptures for more churches explains the multiplicity texts and therefore the survival of the copied texts of the New Testament.

New Testament history: from Bethlehem to Patmos

Unlike the Qur'an, which contains words of teaching from Allah but no narrative, there is a historical narrative running throughout the New Testament. It begins with the birth of Jesus at Bethlehem in about 6 BC and ends with John in exile on the island of Patmos in about AD 95. Between those poles we read of John's baptism of Jesus, his teaching and miracles in Galilee and the final journey to Jerusalem. Each Gospel devotes disproportionate space to Jesus' last few days in Jerusalem.

Within the next decades we learn of congregations of believers, first in the land of Israel but then throughout the countries surrounding the Mediterranean. The letters of the New Testament, including Revelation as a circular letter to seven churches (written mid-90s), are 'historical' documents because they contain details about people, specific circumstances and places.

As I will point out, these Gospels and letters are at many points rooted in known history and geography, contrary to the claims of the New Atheists. The first hundred years of Christianity, when viewed from a wide angle from Jesus to Ignatius, reveals a 'big picture' that fits well into the life and times of the Greco-Roman world of that era.

By contrast, the New Atheists find fault with details and then make negative generalizations about Christianity overall. In the following pages I will answer many, but perhaps not all, of these criticisms. However, the place to begin a defence of 'gospel' truth is not with claimed problematic details but with the unproblematic 'big picture', which includes the verifiable narrative of the New Testament, from Bethlehem to Patmos.

A mission movement focused on Christ

Despite the importance of leaders such as James, Peter, John and Paul, the focus of their literature for their mission networks is not themselves, but Jesus. The Gospels direct our attention to Jesus of Nazareth, Son of Man, Messiah and Son of God, his teachings and miracles, his death and resurrection. The book of Acts and the letters of the apostles are all about the heavenly Lord, his expectations of his people and his return.

The documents are, in effect, 'artefacts' whose existence and character invites explanation. Who or what prompted their creation? Was it a non-person, as Hitchens and others maintain? This is barely worth consideration, especially because of the brevity of the 'lead time' between a non-Jesus and twenty-seven pieces of literature about him. If there was a Jesus, was he 'nothing but' a charismatic holy man or a prophet of some kind? This 'nothing buttery' in turn raises the question how we get from such a lesser figure to the figure in the earliest documents who is already the Christ, the Son of God and the Lord? The texts of the New Testament are 'effects' for which Jesus was the 'cause'. How else can we explain the literature and movement that created it, if it was not Jesus that provided its impetus?

Along with many others I believe Galatians was written in about AD 48, that is, a mere decade and a half after Jesus. Accordingly this letter is our earliest window into Christianity, its tenets and mission:

> Paul, an apostle – not from men nor through man, but through Jesus Christ and *God the Father, who raised him from the dead* – and all the brothers who are with me, To the churches of Galatia: Grace to you and peace from God our Father and *the Lord Jesus Christ, who gave himself for our sins* to deliver us from the present evil age, according to the will of our God and Father, to whom be the glory for ever and ever. Amen. (Gal. 1:1–5)

> But when the fullness of time had come, God sent forth *his Son, born of woman*, born under the law, *to redeem* those who were under the law, so that we might receive adoption as sons. And because you are sons, God has sent *the Spirit of his Son* into our hearts, crying, '*Abba! Father!*' (Gal. 4:4–6)

It is interesting to set these words alongside those of Ignatius quoted above and written sixty years later. Whilst these texts have differing emphases, both point to Jesus as *the Son* whom God sent into the world as *the redeemer*, who was *born of a woman*, and whom *the Father raised from the dead*.

Does Ignatius make a 'god' out of a mere man? Does Paul? Already, just fifteen years after the crucifixion, Paul was reminding these Gentiles in the interior of Asia Minor that the man born of a woman, who was the Son of God, was the risen redeemer. So why did the former persecutor say this unless it was true?

Conclusion

The New Atheists tend to ignore the 'big picture' of the rise and development of early Christianity, preferring to grab hold of apparently awkward details that demonstrate the fatal flaws of the faith they are attacking.

I will address the most important of these details in the following chapters. For now, however, our purpose has been to stand back and see early Christianity from a wide angle of seventy years, between Jesus (died AD 33) and Ignatius' letters (AD 110).

Within that seventy-year time frame, from near its beginning in AD 48 (Galatians) to its end in AD 110 (Ignatius' letters) we are confronted with the same heightened view of Jesus as the resurrected Messiah and Son of God. This was the view of Ignatius, as it was of Matthew, Mark, Luke and John before him; as it was also in the very early letter to the Galatians before them; as it was of every other letter by Paul, James, Peter and John. We reasonably conclude that this was also the view of Jesus himself, which was powerfully confirmed to the early disciples by his resurrection from the dead.

So we must not let the New Atheists seize small pieces of skin, which they believe to be faulty, to rip apart the substantial body of history and theology represented by the body of texts we call the New Testament. The powerful testimony of history will not allow them to do that.

3. HOSTILE WITNESSES TO JESUS

I am a scientist and a believer, and I find no conflict between those world views.

Francis Collins

Christopher Hitchens, one of the most prominent New Atheists, asserted that there is 'no firm evidence whatever that Jesus was a "character in history"',[1] and that there was 'little or no evidence for the life of Jesus'.[2] This is an absolutely unsustainable view and it is no surprise that other atheists are more cautious than Hitchens in this.

I do not know of any respected academic in the field of ancient history, atheist or Christian, who would endorse Hitchens's denial of the historical Jesus. The New Atheists point to G. A. Wells in support of their claims of Jesus' non-existence; but Wells is not a historian.[3]

The strongest evidence for Jesus is to be found in the New

---

1. C. Hitchens, *God Is Not Great: How Religion Poisons Everything* (New York: Twelve, 2007), p. 115.
2. Ibid., p. 127.
3. See G. A. Wells, *The Jesus Myth* (Chicago: Open Court, 1999), p. 103.

Testament, but because many regard this evidence as too biased I will discuss the non-Christian sources instead.

These sources do more than merely establish Jesus as a figure of history. They confirm both the New Testament's 'big picture' historical narrative and its 'big picture' theological understanding of Jesus.

The three earliest non-Christian witnesses to Jesus the Christ (Messiah) and the early Christians are Josephus, Tacitus and Pliny. We are interested to know how these writers think about Christ and Christians. Are they sympathetic or hostile? Do they contradict or corroborate what we find in the writings of the earliest Christians?

Josephus

Born *c.* 37 of aristocratic parents in Jerusalem Josephus became the military leader defending Galilee from the invading Romans AD 66–67 but was captured by the future emperor, General Vespasian. Throughout the remainder of the war he served Vespasian and his son Titus as interpreter and adviser. After the war Vespasian adopted Josephus as a member of the Flavian dynasty, so he became known as *Flavius* Josephus. Vespasian and his sons, the future emperors Titus and Domitian, supported Josephus in a villa in Rome and provided him with financial support to write his propagandist work the *Jewish War*.

In the 90s Josephus wrote his massive history of the Jewish people, *Jewish Antiquities*, where he mentions Jesus and his brother James:

> About this time there lived *Jesus*, a wise man [if indeed one ought to call him a man]. For he was one who wrought surprising feats and was a teacher of such people who accept the truth gladly. He won over many Jews and many of the Greeks. [He was the Christ]. When Pilate, upon hearing him accused by men of the highest standing amongst us had condemned him to be crucified, those who had in the first place come

to love him did not give up their affection for him. [On the third day
he appeared to them restored to life, for the prophets of God had
prophesied these and countless other marvellous things about him.]
And the tribe of Christians, so called after him, has still to this day
not disappeared.[4]

Ananus thought he had a favourable opportunity because Festus was
dead and Albinus was still on his way. So he convened the judges of the
Sanhedrin and brought before them a man named *James*, the brother of
Jesus who was called Christ, and certain others. He accused them of
having transgressed the law and delivered them up to be stoned. Those
of the inhabitants of the city who were considered the most fair-minded
and who were strict in observance of the law were offended at this. They
therefore secretly sent to king Agrippa urging him, for Ananus had not
even been correct in his first step . . . King Agrippa, because of Ananus'
actions, deposed him from the high priesthood . . .[5]

The 'James' passage states that Jesus was 'called Christ' or 'said
to be Christ', which calls into question the 'Jesus' passage that
declares without qualification that Jesus 'was the Christ'. This
suggests the Jesus passage may have been interpolated with extrane-
ous words about Jesus, as bracketed in the 'Jesus' passage above.
The third-century Christian writer Origen specifically stated that
Josephus did not regard Jesus as the Messiah. Yet the text as it stands
above appears in the Christian historian Eusebius' writing of the
first quarter of the fourth century. It seems a Christian enhanced
Josephus' 'Jesus' text some time between Origen and Eusebius.

The 'James' passage appears to be free of interpolation. When
we remove the interpolations from the 'Jesus' passage and consider
it with the 'James' passage, we discover useful information about
Jesus:

4. Josephus, *Jewish Antiquities*, tr. L. H. Feldman, LCL (Cambridge, Mass.;
Heinemann, 1965), 18.63–64, italics added.
5. Ibid., 20.200–201, 203, italics added.

1. Jesus was a rabbi (a 'wise' man) of some kind, who worked
   miracles.
2. He was *said to be* the Messiah, i.e. by his followers.
3. He was executed by Pilate (AD 26–36) at the request of
   leading Jews.
4. Jesus had a brother named James (executed by the high priest
   in 62).
5. 'The tribe of Christians' had not died out when Josephus
   wrote in the 90s.

Josephus' words are a true reflection of the things he would have
observed about early Christianity as a young man in Palestine who
later lived in Rome, where the Christians survived Nero's assault on
them AD 64–65 (see below). Josephus clearly is no Christian, yet he
accurately portrays Christ, his execution and the survival of Christianity.

Tacitus

Cornelius Tacitus (*c.* 56–120) served as consul in Rome in 97 and
proconsul of Roman Asia (112–113). His major work the *Annals of
Imperial Rome* covers the eras of the emperors Tiberius, Gaius, Claudius
and Nero in eighteen books, of which only some parts have survived,
that is, books 1–4, 6 (Tiberius) and 11–16 (Claudius and Nero).

The passage following is part of his lengthy account of the fire
in AD 64 that raged for six days, leaving only four of the fourteen
districts of Rome intact (*Ann.* 15.38–45). In the weeks after the fire
many believed Nero had ordered the torching of the city so as to
rebuild it on a grand scale. Because the rumours about him persisted,
Nero arrested, tried and executed the numerous members of the
Christian sect to deflect attention away from him:

> But neither human help, nor imperial munificence, nor all the modes of
> placating Heaven could stifle or dispel the belief that the fire had taken
> place by order.

Therefore, to scotch the rumour, Nero substituted as culprits, and punished with the utmost refinements of cruelty, a class of men, loathed for their vices, whom the crowd styled Christians.

Christ, the founder of the name, had undergone the death penalty in the reign of Tiberius, by sentence of the procurator Pontius Pilate, and a pernicious superstition was checked for the moment, only to break out once more, not merely in Judea, the home of the disease, but in the capital itself, where all things horrible or shameful in the world collect and find a vogue.

First, then, the confessed members of the sect were arrested; next, on their disclosures, vast numbers were convicted, not so much on the count of arson as for hatred of the human race.

And derision accompanied their end; they were covered with wild beasts' skins and torn to death by dogs; or they were fastened on crosses, and when daylight failed were burned to serve as lamps by night.

Nero had offered his Gardens for the spectacle, and gave an exhibition in his Circus, mingling with the crowd in the habit of a charioteer, or mounted on his car. Hence, in spite of a guilt which had earned the most exemplary punishment, there arose a sentiment of pity, due to the impression that they were being sacrificed not for the welfare of the state but the ferocity of a single man.[6]

As a former consul in Rome, Tacitus would have had access to official archives and may have seen Pilate's report to Tiberius about the execution of Jesus and others in Judea in AD 33. Tacitus' account, which appears not to have been corrupted, contains important information:

1. Christians in Rome were scapegoats for Nero following the fire in AD 64 that destroyed most of Rome.
2. Tacitus says 'vast numbers' of these Christians were convicted, though not for arson but for 'hatred of the human

---

6. Tacitus, *Annals of Imperial Rome*, tr. M. Grant (Harmondsworth: Penguin Classics, 1985), 15.44.

race', a probable reference to their refusal to acknowledge the
primacy of Rome and her Caesar.

3. Although these *Christians* were hated for their 'vices'
   (especially their nonconformity to Roman religious practices),
   the population felt sorry for them.

4. Nero had large numbers crucified, daubed with tar and set
   alight.

5. Tacitus digresses briefly to explain that (a) the *Christians* took
   their name from a certain *Christ* (a Jew?), (b) who was
   executed in Judea under Pontius Pilate, but (c) surprisingly
   Christ's movement (a Jewish sect?) 'broke out afresh' in Judea,
   and (d) his following spread from Judea to Rome. (Tacitus'
   version innocently confirms the resurrection-based 'breakout'
   narrated in the early chapters of the Acts of the Apostles.)

Tacitus is no Christian, yet his onlooker's hostile information
coincides with the New Testament's portrayal of Jesus as one whose
followers proclaimed him to be the Christ, who was executed under
Pilate but whose movement 'broke out afresh' and spread from
Judea to Rome. Tacitus innocently corroborates the raw facts of the
origin and spread of the first three decades of Christianity.

Pliny the Younger

Pliny the Younger (*c.* 61–112), formerly a consul in Rome, was sent
c. 110 by Trajan Caesar to govern the disorganized province of
Bithynia (south of the Black Sea). His correspondence with Trajan
in AD 110–112 is recorded in book 10 of his *Letters*.

In *Letter* 96 he reports the rapid spread of Christianity in the
province in both rural and urbanized areas. Temples were abandoned
and the businesses of those who sold fodder for sacrificial animals
had been shut down through lack of demand.

Pliny interrogated those accused of being Christians and
sentenced them to death if they insisted on saying they were such,

despite being asked the question three times. The governor dispatched those who were Roman citizens to Rome for trial.

Some non-citizens who were accused acknowledged they had been Christians but no longer were. Pliny subjected them to a formal legal procedure. They were required to pray to the state gods according to Pliny's dictated statement, engage in an act of worship with incense to the emperor's image and also 'curse Christ'. Pliny's was a two-pronged attack involving affirmation of the gods and the denial of Christ.

Pliny twice refers to Christ, but without further explanation. We reasonably assume that Pliny knew that Christ had been executed in Judea some years before but did not need to tell Trajan. Since his friend Tacitus, governor of neighbouring Asia, made this clear (as noted above), we assume it was common knowledge among Roman emperors and bureaucrats:

> They maintained that their guilt or error had amounted only to this:
> they had been in the habit of meeting on an appointed day before
> daybreak and singing a hymn antiphonally to Christ as if to a god,
> and binding themselves with an oath – not to commit any crime but
> to abstain from theft, robbery, and adultery, from breach of faith, and
> from repudiating a trust when called upon to honour it. After this
> ceremony, it had been their custom to disperse and reassemble to take
> food of a harmless kind . . . [7]

Pliny provides us with useful information about early Christianity and Christian practices:

1. Christians had become very numerous in Bithynia since at least AD 90, so much so that many pagan temples had been closed.

---

7. Pliny, *Epistle*, tr. M. Harris, 'References to Jesus in Early Classical Authors', in D. Wenham (ed.), *Gospel Perspectives* (Sheffield: JSOT, 1984), vol. 5, p. 345 (10.96.7).

2. Their practices included meeting on a fixed day and chanting hymns to Christ 'as if *to* a god', confirming very early New Testament texts that Christians met to worship Christ, including by singing hymns *to* him as Lord (e.g. *Maran atha*, 'Come back, Lord'; 1 Cor. 16:22).

3. Christians viewed Christ above the emperor and the gods, and would die rather than comply with Roman 'tests' of praying to statues of the emperor and the gods and cursing Christ.

Pliny the outside observer is deeply opposed to the Christians. Nonetheless his portrayal of their dedication to Christ and their religious meetings is consistent with the Christians' own version of these things, as we find them in the New Testament.

Conclusion

Important conclusions arise from our review of Josephus, Tacitus and Pliny.

First, they are important witnesses to the fact of Jesus' existence and the spread of early Christianity. That importance is enhanced because they were 'outsiders', non-Christians. Two of them – Tacitus and Pliny – are pointedly hostile to the Christian movement; Josephus' account is more neutral. Hitchens's scepticism is unsustainable in the face of sources that are independent and in two cases hostile.

Secondly, at no point of detail do these sources contradict historical details in the New Testament; rather they confirm its 'raw' facts about the origin of Christianity in Judea and its rapid spread throughout the empire. Tacitus' account of the execution of Christ in Judea under Pilate (AD 26–36) endorses the Gospels' account of the execution of Jesus in Jerusalem. His account of the killing of multitudes of Christians in Rome under Nero in the mid-60s is consistent with a letter of Paul addressing Christians in Rome (AD 57) and the Acts narrative where Paul meets Christians in southern Italy (AD 60).

Pliny's letter to Trajan about Christians in Bithynia confirms the first letter of Peter that was addressed to believers in five Roman provinces in Asia Minor, including Bithynia. The secular sources support the New Testament's macro-history.

Thirdly, these writers also confirm the New Testament's exalted view of Jesus, although they do not share that view. It is striking that Josephus, Tacitus and Pliny each use *Christ* as a name, as the New Testament letters also frequently do. Yet it is evident from the Gospels that 'Christ' was initially a title, '*the* Christ' (which is Greek for '*the* Messiah'). The transition from a title to a name probably occurred because Gentiles would have been bewildered by reference to someone as 'the smeared one' (which 'the Christ' literally means). This explains how the title 'the Christ' became a surname, 'Christ'. Nonetheless the consistent non-Christian use of the words 'Christ' and 'Christian' preserve the original meaning of Jesus as *the* Messiah, whose followers were dubbed 'Messiah's men', 'Christians'. That the non-Christian witnesses never speak of 'Jesus' men' is also significant.

Of great importance is Pliny's window into early Christian meetings, where people assembled weekly to worship this crucified man *as if alive, as if to a god*. Pliny confirms the central claims of the New Testament that, although Jesus of Nazareth was crucified as the Messiah, his followers gathered to worship him as the risen Lord. Pliny's they sang 'a hymn . . . to Christ *as if to a god*' exactly confirms Paul's injunction 'singing and making melody to the Lord with your heart' (Eph. 5:19). For Pliny the Roman Trajan Caesar was god, so that for these Christians to worship Christ 'as if a god' was blasphemous, treasonable and worthy of death.

Evidence from these non-Christian sources about Christ and Christianity makes unsustainable Hitchens's assertion of Jesus' non-existence.

4. THE IMMEDIATE IMPACT OF JESUS

The New Atheists are quick to seize on perceived discrepancies within the New Testament (see chapter 7) but they do not display much understanding of the notion of 'cause and effect' within the stream of history. The British establishment of a penal settlement in New South Wales in 1788 was the demonstrable result not only of Cook's exploration of its coastline in 1770, but also of the loss of penal colonies in North America through the American War of Independence (1775–83).[1] James Cook discovered New South Wales (1770), the British lost a place to locate their swollen prison population to in America (1783), and they established a new penal colony in New South Wales (beginning in 1788). The notion of causation is evident. By analogy, the early rise of Christianity beginning in AD 33 is to be attributed to the direct and immediate impact of the public ministry of Jesus (AD 29–33).

---

1. Over fifty thousand British convicts were sent to colonial America during the eighteenth century.

Incidental evidence from two early letters

Geoffrey Elton (1921–94), the great historian of Tudor England, made a critical distinction between '[evidence] produced specifically for the [historian's] attention and that produced for another purpose'.[2] Whilst Elton was applying this critical principle to his own field of study it is no less relevant to the historical study of the origin of Christianity.

The Gospels and the Acts of the Apostles fit into Elton's first category, comprising 'in the main, evidence of a literary and often secondary kind: chronicles, memoirs, notes of self-justification, letters intended for publication'.[3] According to Elton, those produced 'for another purpose' included trivia such as invoices and personal letters. Nonetheless these unpromising sources often yield valuable social and economic data for the modern historian. The letters of the New Testament belong to Elton's second category, items 'created for another purpose', that is, 'the ordinary products of life'.[4]

Whereas the Gospels and Acts were, as it were, *formal* records about Jesus and the early history of the church,[5] the letters of Paul are *incidental* documents addressing current issues in the churches, 'the ordinary products of life', documents not consciously 'intended

---

2. G. R. Elton, *The Practice of History* (Sydney: Sydney University Press, 1967), p. 77.
3. Ibid.
4. Ibid.
5. It would be incorrect to assume that Matthew, Mark, Luke and John did not have pastoral settings in mind when they wrote for their churches. Indeed they did, but those contexts are mostly to be implied and are thus open to debate. Their situation is complicated by our difficulty in the dating and provenance of their texts, or, for that matter, the location of their readers. The writers of the letters, however, are relatively direct in stating the circumstances of the churches or individuals to whom they wrote. Furthermore, at least in the case of Paul's letters and 1 Peter, we are mostly confident about questions of dating, provenance and location.

for publication'. Paul's letters dealt with the mundane issues affecting the churches and his own frequently difficult relationships with them. These letters are innocent of any attempt to convey new information about the historical Jesus or about the circumstances by which the message of Christianity came to the churches. These things his readers already knew.

Paul's information about Jesus and early Christian history, therefore, is especially valuable, for two reasons. First, it is – as noted – incidental and gratuitous, and therefore not able to be challenged as contrived for apologetic purposes in later generations. Secondly, Paul's letters are the earliest documents of Christianity and are the evidence that is historically the closest to Jesus and the earliest churches. When we begin with the letters of Paul – in particular Galatians and 1 Corinthians[6] – we are able to begin at the beginning, at the source of the earliest evidence.

Galatians

Paul wrote to the Galatian churches (in central Asia Minor) from Antioch in Syria in *c.* 48.[7] He devotes the first two chapters to defending the independence and integrity of God's commission of him as his apostle to the Gentiles. Whilst he gives due recognition to James, Cephas (Peter) and John, the leaders of the church in Jerusalem, he insists that he acts under God's authority, not theirs.

In the course of these arguments defending his autonomy Paul mentions in passing several details about Christianity in Jerusalem at the time. He acknowledges that he had 'persecuted' and 'attempted to destroy' the 'church of God' in Jerusalem (Gal. 1:13). Based on

---

6. 1 Thessalonians was written in AD 50 or 51 and contains material that supports the argument of this chapter, but for reasons of brevity it is not included.

7. See F. F. Bruce, *Commentary on Galatians*, NIGTC (Grand Rapids: Eerdmans, 1982), pp. 1–18. Many scholars, however, argue that Paul wrote the letter in the middle 50s from Ephesus or Corinth. The arguments of this chapter are not affected in principle by this dating a few years later.

AD 33 as the date of the crucifixion it would mean that these persecutions by Paul occurred later in 33 or in 34. The point is that from a gratuitous reference in a letter written in AD 48 we have evidence of the existence of the 'church of God' in the immediate aftermath of the lifespan of Jesus. The idea of the 'church' was not a later ecclesiastical construct but an entity whose foundation is reasonably to be attributed to Jesus.

Furthermore Paul notes that three years after the Damascus event (i.e. in AD 36/37) he returned to Jerusalem, where he met the 'apostles' Cephas and James, the 'brother of the Lord' (Gal. 1:18–19). From these gratuitous references we have secure evidence of the existence of the 'office' of 'apostle' within four years of Jesus' lifespan, whose prime holder was Cephas, the leading disciple of Jesus according to the Gospels. Again, the evidence points to Jesus, who appointed Cephas and others as 'apostles' (which means 'sent ones').

Thus Galatians provides 'cause and effect' evidence whereby the 'effects' were 'the church of God' (in Jerusalem) and leaders known as 'apostles'. If these were the 'effects', their 'cause' was Jesus; and 'cause' and 'effect' were separated by a very brief space of time, at most four years.

How does this information 'produced for another purpose' (in a letter to the wayward Galatian churches) relate to '[evidence] produced specifically for the [historian's] attention' (in the Acts of the Apostles)? The passing references in Galatians about 'the church of God', the 'apostles' and 'Cephas and James' exactly confirm the formal information about the church and the apostles in the book of Acts.

From these data we draw the conclusion that Jesus 'caused' an immediate impact: (1) the creation of a body called 'the church of God', and (2) church leaders known as 'apostles', two of whom are named.

Galatians is noteworthy in another respect. As noted earlier (chapter 2) this early letter expresses a 'high' view of Jesus. Some authorities refer to the idea of evolution or 'development' over time to explain the later church's high view of Jesus. This suggests that

the 'real' Jesus was a mere rabbi or prophet but who, with the passage
of time, became inflated by his followers as a deity figure.

Paul wrote Galatians only fifteen years after Jesus, about whom
he states:

> when the fullness of time had come,
> God sent forth *his Son*,
>> born of woman,
>> born under the law,
> to *redeem* those who were under the law,
> so that we might receive adoption as sons.
> And because you are sons,
> God has sent *the Spirit of his Son* into our hearts,
>> crying, '*Abba*! *Father*!' (Gal. 4:4–6)

It would take many pages to draw out the meaning of these few yet
weighty words about Jesus. Such is their brevity, yet also their
symmetry, that we think they were some kind of creed Paul had
created, either during his decade ministering in Syria and Cilicia (Gal.
1:21–24) or more recently on an ad hoc basis for the needs of his
Galatian readers. Either way, Paul's words dispel any notion of an
evolutionary development of a view of Jesus from a lower to a
higher form.

Perhaps, though, these opinions about Jesus were only the
opinions of Paul, a renegade who took Christianity in directions
neither Jesus nor his disciples intended? That, at least, is how many
regard Paul. Galatians itself, however, indicates that such a view is
historically unlikely if not unsustainable, for three reasons.

First, the raw convert Paul had extensive opportunity to learn
about Jesus from Cephas, with whom he 'enquired' when he
'remained' with him for fifteen days, and from James, the brother of
the Lord, whom he also 'saw' in Jerusalem (Gal. 1:18–19). In other
words, in 36/37 Paul had extensive opportunity to learn about Jesus
of Nazareth from his brother James and about the ministry, teachings,
death and resurrection of Jesus from Cephas, the leading disciple.

Secondly, a decade later, after Paul's extensive evangelism in Syria and Cilicia, he revisited Jerusalem to secure the goodwill of James, Cephas and John ('pillars' of the Jerusalem church) to 'go' to the Gentiles. In the course of this visit these apostolic leaders 'added nothing' to the doctrines Paul rehearsed before them (Gal. 2:2, 6), and they did not require the 'Greek' Titus to be circumcised. Faith in Christ crucified was more than sufficient to 'justify' Titus before God and to qualify him fully as a true covenant brother. In other words, the doctrines Paul had been teaching in Syria–Cilicia (AD 37–47), and which are echoed throughout Galatians (AD 48), were entirely consistent with the doctrines of the three men who headed the parallel mission to the Jews.

Thirdly, Paul had a number of serious critics in the Galatian churches who would have seized on any misstatement or exaggeration and would have used it against him with his pro-circumcision critics in the Jerusalem church. This is good reason to regard Paul's words as accurate.

In short, the 'weighty' words about Jesus (Gal. 4:4–6) were written within the brief period after Jesus and they would have met with the approval of the apostolic leaders in Jerusalem, two of whom (Cephas and John) had been disciples of the historical Jesus. From the beginning of Christian history, and not just later, Jesus was regarded as the Son of God, a member of the divine Trinity and the Redeemer. Furthermore in the years to come Cephas and John were to write about Jesus, which they also did in their own words but in no less exalted terms (see e.g. 1 Pet. 1:17–21; John 1:1–18).

1 Corinthians

Paul wrote '1 Corinthians' early in AD 55, a second 'follow-up' letter after his formation of the church in the city of Corinth in AD 50–52.[8]

---

8. Paul wrote the first 'follow-up' letter (called the 'previous' letter) to deal with disciplinary problems some time between his departure from Corinth (AD 52) and the writing of 1 Corinthians (AD 55).

Whilst the focus of this letter is on various current ethical and doctrinal issues in the church in Corinth, Paul also mentions in passing a number of historical events (see figure 4.1 below).

29–33	33	34	34 or 36	34–50	50
The Lord's teachings about marriage and the payment of ministers (7:10; 9:14)	The Lord's institution of the remembrance meal at the Last Supper (11:23–26)	The Lord 'appeared' to Paul, entrusting him with a 'stewardship' (15:8; 9:17)	Paul 'received' the 'tradition' about death, burial, resurrection and appearances of Christ (15:3–7)	Paul worked 'harder' (than other apostles) in preaching the gospel (15:10)	Paul preached the gospel in Corinth and established the church (15:1)

Fig. 4.1 Timeline: between Jesus and Paul in Corinth.

Paul arrived in Corinth in AD 50, about seventeen years after the crucifixion and resurrection of Jesus.

During those seventeen years a number of confessional-type statements were formulated about Jesus. One respected scholar goes so far as to say that 17% of 1 Corinthians existed as pre-formed statements before Paul wrote the letter (1,142 words from a total of 6,807).[9] It is difficult to be precise about this because Paul is so skilled and versatile a writer. Is a passage a preformed quotation, or just another example of Paul's own rhetorical brilliance summoned for the moment?

There are three passages that depend on the words of the Lord, one relating to marriage, another to payment of ministers and the other citing the words of the Lord at the Last Supper (7:10; 9:14; 11:23–26). Paul's reverend attitude to the Lord's words points to the impact of Jesus on the apostle and through him upon the members of the church in Corinth.

---

9. E. E. Ellis, *The Making of the New Testament Documents* (Leiden: Brill, 2002), p. 94.

There are also a number of passages in 1 Corinthians that appear to have been pre-formulated, which he quotes in the letter.

A catechism

Within a year or so of the resurrection the apostles (presumably) formulated these words as a faith statement that Paul later 'received' and then 'delivered' in Corinth (and no doubt other churches along the way).

> For I *delivered* to you as of first importance
> what I also *received*:
> *that* Christ *died* for our sins in accordance with the Scriptures,
> *that* he was *buried*,
> *that* he was *raised* on the third day in accordance with the
>   Scriptures,

and	*that* he *appeared*	to Cephas,
then		to the twelve.
Then	he appeared	to more than five hundred brothers at one time,
		most of whom are still alive,
		though some have fallen asleep.
Then	he appeared	to James,
then		to all the apostles. (1 Cor. 15:3–7)

This statement was crafted as an early (AD 34?), carefully formulated catechism for the instruction of converts, as the following features show: (1) the terms 'delivered' and 'received' are 'rabbinic' and indicate that authoritative figures had pre-formulated these words; (2) the fourfold 'that' points to the four primary elements in the gospel that Paul himself had 'received' and that he 'delivered' in Corinth;[10] (3) the four verbs portray the 'Easter' event as a single connected entity: he 'appeared' because he had been 'raised'; he was

---

10. The Greek *hoti* (that) introduces words in quotation marks, pointing to key elements in the original message.

'raised' having been 'buried'; he was 'buried' because he had (truly) 'died'; (4) Christ appeared initially to Cephas and this was followed by the fourfold 'then' for a sequence of four sets of 'appearances' to others.

This exceedingly early catechism is historical evidence of the immediate impact of Jesus on his disciples in the aftermath of the first Easter.

Words of knowledge

Paul uses the verb 'know' and the noun 'knowledge' to remind his readers of items of teaching he had imparted when he was present with them (AD 50–52). The following passage is 'framed' by 'we know' (referring to the well-instructed members) and 'not all possess this knowledge' (referring to a 'weak', less well-instructed member: see verses 7–13).

> Therefore, as to the eating of food offered to idols,
> we *know* that 'an idol has no real existence',
> and that 'there is no God but one.'
> For although there may be so-called gods in heaven or on earth
> – as indeed there are many 'gods' and many 'lords' –
> yet for us there is
> one God, the Father,
>> from whom are all things and
>> for whom we exist,
> and one Lord, Jesus Christ,
>> through whom are all things and through whom we exist.
> However, not all possess this *knowledge*. (1 Cor. 8:4–7)

In between these references to 'know' and 'knowledge' is Paul's reminder that 'an idol has no real existence' (negative) and 'there is no God but one' (positive). Against the popular Corinthian perception of 'many "gods" and many "lords"' Paul states the true 'knowledge' that he had taught them, that there is 'one God' and 'one Lord'. This 'one God' is further identified as 'the Father', the source 'from whom all things come' and 'for whom we exist'. This 'one Lord' is further identified as 'Jesus Christ', the agent 'through whom are all things and through whom we exist'.

The symmetry of the passage and its adaptation of the great Jewish confession, the Shema, 'Hear, O Israel: the LORD our God, the LORD is *one*. You shall love the Lord your God . . . ' (Deut. 6:4–5), points to a statement that had been pre-formulated in the seventeen years between Jesus and Paul's arrival in Corinth, whether by Paul or by others.

We note the astonishing impact of Jesus upon the person who constructed this 'word of knowledge' as an adaptation of the Shema. The 'Lord' who is 'one' is 'Jesus Christ' who is now identified with Yahweh, Israel's Lord. The 'God' who is 'one' is now identified as 'the Father', who is the Creator. In other words, such was the impact of Jesus on those Jews who became his followers that they radically redefined the being of God, as previously declared in their most sacred confession (which observant Jews confessed twice daily).[11]

Paul makes one further allusion to the Shema: 'If anyone has no *love* for the Lord [i.e. the Lord *Jesus*] let him be accursed' (1 Cor. 16:22). The Shema called for the love of Yahweh, but Paul called for the love of Jesus the Lord. The mandate to love Jesus has replaced the mandate to love Yahweh, the God of Israel.

This remarkable and emphatically early passage dismisses the theory of the later evolution from a lower to a high view of Jesus. The historical evidence, rather, is that there was a high view of Jesus from the beginning of Christian history, a high view that can reasonably be explained only by the deity and resurrection of Jesus and his impact on his original followers.

---

11. R. Bauckham, *God Crucified: Monotheism and Christology in the New Testament* (Grand Rapids: Eerdmans, 1998), writes, 'Paul has rearranged the words in such a way as to produce an affirmation of both one God, the Father, and one Lord, Jesus Christ. It should be quite clear that Paul is including the Lord Jesus Christ in the unique divine identity' (p. 38).

Conclusion

Galatians and 1 Corinthians, as two early letters, provide clear evidence of the theological impetus created by the historical impact of Jesus, his deity, teaching, crucifixion and resurrection. The challenge to new atheists and other sceptics is to explain these otherwise awkward 'knock-on' effects that are so clearly evident in the early letters. If Jesus was not the 'cause' of these 'effects', we ask, what was? The point is that the New Atheists seize what they see as discrepancies within the New Testament records but display little grasp of the 'cause and effect' character so clearly on view in the records of early Christianity.

5. GOSPEL TRUTH AND WORLD HISTORY

Luke's account [in Luke-Acts] always remains within the limits of what was considered reliable by the standards of antiquity.

Martin Hengel

What if the New Atheists discovered a glaring contradiction between the Gospels and wider history? Would that fatally damage the whole of Christianity? In this chapter I point out that there are several puzzlingly problematic passages in the writings of Luke, one in the Gospel, the other in the Acts of the Apostles. If we had all the information from the period it may be that these are not problems at all, but based on the texts themselves it appears there are issues.

But even if there are problem passages, and the 'if' must be stressed, this would not destroy the edifice of New Testament history from Bethlehem to Patmos. There are problematic issues in all ancient history studies, for that is the nature of those studies. Yet individual problems do not invalidate our overall picture of Herod or Tiberius any more than they do of Jesus and the rise of Christianity.

The historical setting of Matthew, Mark and John

The setting of three of the Gospels – Matthew, Mark and John – is reasonably straightforward. Each Gospel locates John's baptism of

Jesus as the commencement of Jesus' public ministry. John was a famous prophet whose imprisonment and execution Josephus also reports. Matthew and Mark situate the primary ministry of Jesus in the Galilee ruled by Herod Antipas, who had imprisoned John the Baptist. Matthew, Mark and John agree that Jesus came finally to Jerusalem, where he was interrogated by the temple authorities, who handed him over to Pilate for further interrogation prior to his crucifixion. Matthew and Mark highlight the Jewish trial of Jesus, whereas John in his Gospel writes expansively on the Roman trial. Secular sources refer to key New Testament figures such as John the Baptist (by Josephus), Herod Antipas (by Josephus and Philo), Annas and Caiaphas (by Josephus) and Pilate (by Josephus, Philo and Tacitus).

Luke's writings, however, call for more comment. Appended to his Gospel is his second 'book', the Acts of the Apostles, of equal length. Luke's double volume chronicles events from the birth of John the Baptist to the imprisonment of Paul in Rome, a period of about seventy years. Furthermore there are numerous linkages with world history from these texts.

Sceptics seize on two texts as sure evidence of the unreliability of Luke in particular and of the New Testament in general. To anticipate, my argument will be that even if error was to be conceded to Luke-Acts it would not invalidate the global historical picture of Luke's writings or of the New Testament. If such a reductionist approach were adopted regarding other ancient sources, there would be very little that ancient historians could say about other famous people from that era.

Linkages in Luke-Acts

In table 5.1 on pages 58–61 are the linkages Luke makes connecting events and people in his narrative of salvation history with known people and events in world history. In all but two cases Luke's references 'fit' well with details in world history.

Luke's two-volume work covering almost seventy years is impressive. No less so are the many linkages from Luke's history into the complex world history of those seven decades.

The problem passages

Before looking at the problem cases we need to reflect on the sources available to Luke. It is widely believed that Luke was from Antioch in Syria and had become a follower of Christ in the 40s. We know he wrote his two-volume work Luke-Acts dependent in part on *written* texts 'handed over' to him by the first disciples (Luke 1:1–4). The 'we' narratives throughout Acts 21 – 28 indicate that Luke was Paul's companion for about five years (AD 57–62), suggesting that Paul himself had been the *oral* source for Luke's narratives about Paul. The two to three years Luke spent in Palestine in the late 50s would have provided opportunity to glean further *oral* and *written* information about Jesus' birth, boyhood and ministry and the early years of Christianity in Palestine. We do not know who such people were or what written sources may have been available to Luke.

The main problem passage: Luke 2:2

Luke locates the birth of Jesus in the days of Herod (Luke 2:5, 26) and at the time of the census conducted under Quirinius (Luke 2:2). The problem is that Herod died in 4 BC, whereas Josephus plainly tells us that Quirinius' census occurred in AD 6, ten years later. Quirinius was a prominent Roman general who does not appear to have been the governor of Syria before AD 6.[1] It seems Luke has made a significant error by locating Jesus' birth about ten years too late!

---

1. The governors of Syria during this period were M. Titius (10 BC), C. Sentius Saturninus (9–6 BC), Quinctilius Varus (6–4 BC), Calpurnius Piso (4–1 BC), C. Iulius Caesar (1 BC – AD 4), L. Volusius Saturninus (AD 4–5) and P. Sulpicius Quirinius (AD 6). See further E. Schürer, *The History of the Jewish People in the Age of Jesus Christ*, rev. and ed. G. Vermes and F. Millar, vol. 1 (Edinburgh: T. & T. Clark, 1973), pp. 257–259.

Table 5.1 Luke's linkages into world history

Date	Event	Reference	Cross-reference
6 BC	Birth of John the Baptist and therefore of Jesus 'in the days of *Herod*, king of Judea'.	Luke 1:5, 26	Herod was king 40–4 BC and his rule is extensively documented by Josephus, *War* 1.210–673, and *Ant.* 15.1–16.354; cf. Philo, *Flacc.* 25; *Legat.* 294–299; Tacitus, *Ann.* 12.23; *Hist.* 5.4, 9.
AD 6	'In those days a decree went out from Caesar Augustus that all the world should be registered. This was the first registration when Quirinius was governor of Syria.	Luke 2:1–2	'The territory subject to Archelaus was added to Syria and Quirinius ... was sent by Caesar to take a census of property in Syria and to sell the Estate of Archelaus' (Josephus, *Ant.* 17.355).
	'*Judas the Galilean* rose up in the days of the census and drew away some of the people after him. He too perished, and all who followed him were scattered.'	Acts 5:37	'A Galilean ... Judas incited his countrymen to revolt [over] paying tribute to the Romans' (Josephus, *War* 2.118).
AD 28/29	'In the fifteenth year of the reign of Tiberius Caesar, *Pontius Pilate* being governor of Judea, and Herod being tetrarch of Galilee, and his brother Philip tetrarch of the region of Ituraea and Trachonitis ... during the high priesthood of Annas and Caiaphas, the word of God came to *John* ...'	Luke 3:1–2	'the nation was divided into three provinces under the sons of Herod' (Tacitus, *Hist.* 5.9). 'Pilate, being sent by Tiberius as procurator to Judea ...' (Josephus, *War* 2.169). 'Herod [Antipas] put John the Baptist to death though he was a good man' (Josephus, *Ant.* 18.113–117).

AD 33	Luke 23:3	'Pilate asked him [Jesus], "Are you the King of the Jews?"'
		'Christus ... suffered the extreme penalty ... at the hands of Pontius Pilate' (Tacitus, *Ann.* 15.44).
AD 34	Acts 5:36–37	'For before these days *Theudas* rose up, claiming to be somebody, and a number of men, about four hundred, joined him. He was killed, and all who followed him were dispersed and came to nothing. After him *Judas the Galilean* rose up in the days of the census and drew away some of the people after him. He too perished, and all who followed him were scattered.'
		'when Fadus was procurator of Judea [AD 44–46], a certain imposter named Theudas persuaded the majority of the masses to take up their possessions and follow him to the Jordan. He stated that he was a prophet and that at his command the river would be parted ... With this talk he persuaded many ... Theudas himself was captured, whereupon they cut off his head and brought it to Jerusalem' (Josephus, *Ant.* 20.97–89).
		'[In AD 6–7] A Galilean ... Judas incited his countrymen to revolt [over] paying tribute to the Romans' (Josephus, *War* 2.118).
AD 44	Acts 12:21–23	'On an appointed day *Herod* [Agrippa I] put on his royal robes, took his seat upon the throne, and delivered an oration to them. And the people were shouting, "The voice of a god, and not of a man!" Immediately an angel of the Lord struck him down, because he did not give God the glory, and he was eaten by worms and breathed his last.'
		'Clad in a garment woven completely of silver ... he [King Herod Agrippa I] entered the theatre at daybreak ... his flatterers addressed him as a god ... the king did not rebuke them ... [he] felt a stab in his heart ... after five days he departed this life' (Josephus, *Ant.* 19.344–349).

Date	Event	Reference	Cross-reference
AD 44–45	'Agabus . . . foretold by the Spirit that there would be a great *famine* over all the world (this took place in the days of Claudius).'	Acts 11:28	'It was in the administration of Tiberius Alexander [AD 46–48] that the great famine occurred in Judea' (Josephus, *Ant.* 20.101).
AD 49	'After this Paul left Athens and went to Corinth. And he found a Jew named Aquila, a native of Pontus, recently come from Italy with his wife Priscilla, because Claudius had commanded all the Jews to leave Rome.'	Acts 18:1–2	'Since the Jews constantly made disturbances at the instigation of Chrestus he [Claudius] expelled them from Rome' (Suetonius, *Claud.* 25.4).
AD 51	'But when *Gallio* was proconsul of Achaia . . .'	Acts 18:12	See the Inscription at Delphi, which fixes Gallio's appointment to Achaia in AD 51(?).
AD 57	'When we had come to Jerusalem . . . Paul went in with us to *James*, and all the elders were present.'	Acts 21:17–18	'[In AD 62] Ananus [Annas II] convened the judges of the Sanhedrin and brought before them James, the brother of Jesus who is called Christ . . . to be stoned' (Josephus, *Ant.* 20.200).
AD 57	'Are you not *the Egyptian*, then, who recently stirred up a revolt and led the four thousand men of the Assassins out into the wilderness?'	Acts 21:38	'The Egyptian false prophet . . . collected a following of about 30,000 dupes and led them . . . from the desert to the Mount of Olives' (Josephus, *War* 2.261).
AD 57	'And the high priest *Ananias* commanded those who stood by him to strike him [Paul] on the mouth.'	Acts 23:2	'Herod King of Chalcis . . . assigned the office [of high priest] to Ananias . . .' (Josephus, *Ant.* 20.103).

AD 58	Acts 24:24	'At the time when Felix was procurator of Judea [Drusilla] married Felix . . .' (Josephus, *Ant.* 20.131–143; cf. Tacitus, *Hist.* 5.9; *Ann.* 12.54).
		'After some days Felix came with his wife Drusilla, who was Jewish, and he sent for Paul and heard him speak about faith in Christ Jesus.'	
AD 60	Acts 24:27	'When Porcius Festus was sent by Nero as successor to Felix . . .' (Josephus, *Ant.* 20.182).
		'When two years had elapsed, Felix was succeeded by Porcius Festus. And desiring to do the Jews a favour, Felix left Paul in prison.'	
AD 60	Acts 25:13	'Bernice lived for a long time as a widow. But when the report gained currency that she had a liaison with her brother [Agrippa] she induced Polemo king of Cilicia to be circumcised and take her in marriage' (Josephus, *Ant.* 20.145).
		'Now when some days had passed, Agrippa [II] the king and Bernice arrived at Caesarea and greeted Festus.'	

There are four possible explanations.

The first is that Luke innocently replicated an error in the written or oral information he had received. Against this, however, is Luke's clear understanding that Herod's realm had been divided after his death (Luke 3:1–2) and, therefore, that Joseph from Galilee would have paid his taxes in Galilee, so there would have been no need for him to travel to Bethlehem in Judea to be registered for paying taxes in that jurisdiction. This explanation is unlikely.

The second is that Luke deliberately introduced the error to make the theological point that he favoured the uprising led by Judas. This is unsustainable since the only point Luke makes is to contrast the humble godliness of little, defenceless people such as Joseph, Mary, the infant Jesus and the shepherds with the distant, uncaring figure of Caesar Augustus, whose decree brought such suffering.

A third explanation is that the error lies with Josephus. Whilst there are some discrepancies between Josephus' *Jewish War* and his *Jewish Antiquities*, any theory of error in this matter is unlikely. Quirinius' census was a momentous event marking the radical transition from Judea as a Jewish ethnarchy under Archelaus to a Roman province under its first prefect, Coponius. The imposition of direct Roman rule in Judea meant the imposition of a tax now payable directly to Caesar, symbolizing that he, not God was the 'master' of the people. It was this 'numbering' of the people that drove Judas to lead his rebellion (Acts 5:37; cf. Num. 1:2). That census provoked the rebellion which began the troubles that eventually issued in the catastrophic Roman conquest of Palestine in AD 66–70. Twenty-seven years after the initial rebellion the census was still a burning issue, inspiring the loaded question to Jesus 'Is it lawful to pay taxes to Caesar, or not?' (Mark 12:14).

The fourth explanation is that there was an earlier census but that Luke's very brief sentence (only nine words) blurs the issue. The critical word is 'first' (*prōtos*). Grammar experts argue that 'first' in

Luke 2:2 is an adjective meaning 'first' in a superlative sense (first of at least three).[2]

There is, however, an insurmountable historical problem in insisting that 'first' must be understood as a superlative sense. It implies that there were at least *two other* censuses in Judea *after* Quirinius' famous census in AD 6. Quirinius' census was a momentous event that provoked a rebellion, which Luke elsewhere rightly called *the* census (Acts 5:37). Had there been other subsequent censuses in Palestine after Quirinius we would know about them from Josephus, so controversial were they.

Also note that the word 'first' can also mean 'foremost', or 'most prominent', that is, in an absolute sense. By way of example, the prodigal son's father commanded, 'bring . . . the *best* robe' (Luke 15:22), and the scribe asked Jesus, 'Which commandment is the *greatest* of all?' (Mark 12:28). This use of 'first' meaning 'foremost' in an *absolute* sense is a genuine alternative to understanding 'first' in a *superlative* sense (first of at least three). Understood in this way, Luke 2:2 would read as, 'This enrolment became most prominent when Quirinius was governor of Syria.' In other words, the historically minded Luke is making a merely passing reference to this famous event.

But that event was not the occasion of the journey of Joseph and Mary to Bethlehem. Luke's words, in effect, distinguish the enrolment during Herod's reign involving Joseph and Mary from the 'most prominent' later enrolment under Quirinius in AD 6. This would mean that Luke 2:2 is alluding to an otherwise unknown enrolment during Herod's time, when his kingdom was undivided, and when Joseph of the line of David, was required to enrol in Bethlehem, his ancestral city.

Some argue against the historical possibility of a census earlier than Quirinius' census. Yet we know that Augustus conducted an

---

2. Yet Luke uses the same Greek adjective in Acts 1:1 in a *comparative* (*non-superlative*) sense, where the 'first book' clearly means *the first of two* books, i.e., 'the *former* book' (Luke's Gospel).

imperial census beginning in 18 BC (*Res gest. divi Aug.* 8) and that such
a census could have occurred within the domain of a client king
such as Herod (Tacitus, *Ann.* 6.41).[3] Furthermore there is evidence
of a Roman registration in Egypt in 104 BC requiring registrants to
return to their ancestral homes.[4] We know also that Augustus Caesar
required the 'whole Jewish people' in Israel to make an oath of
allegiance to him in about 7 BC (Josephus, *Ant.* 17.42), though there
is no information about a necessity for Jews to return to their
ancestral cities.[5]

Luke 2:2 has been the subject of hundreds of scholarly books and
articles, but the problems remain unsolved. It seems Luke has either
replicated an error from the sources available to him, or, more
probably, has expressed himself rather too briefly. There is a strong
possibility of an enrolment during Herod's years that could have
affected Joseph and Mary. Either way it would be unreasonable to
accuse Luke of wilful error, for what would have been his reason for
doing so? I do not think the problems in Luke 2:2 are a basis for the
wholesale rejection of this author, his integrity or competence.

The second problem passage: Acts 5:35–39

The incident Luke reports occurred within a year after the first
Easter. The apostles faced execution for persisting in preaching
about Christ in Jerusalem. At a meeting of the supreme council
the eminent Pharisee Gamaliel, the teacher of Paul, cautioned
against this:

> Men of Israel, take care what you are about to do with these men. For
> before these days Theudas rose up, claiming to be somebody, and a
> number of men, about four hundred, joined him. He was killed, and all

---

3. For examples of censuses being conducted in 'vassal kingdoms' (e.g.
   Apamea, Cappadocia, Petra and Samaria) see H. Hoehner, *Chronological
   Aspects of the Life of Christ* (Grand Rapids: Zondervan, 1977), p. 16.
4. Ibid., p. 15.
5. P. W. Barnett, 'Enrolment in Luke 2:1–5', *ExpTim* 55.12 (1974),
   pp. 374–380.

who followed him were dispersed and came to nothing. After him Judas
the Galilean rose up in the days of the census and drew away some
of the people after him. He too perished, and all who followed him were
scattered. So in the present case I tell you, keep away from these men and
let them alone, for if this plan or this undertaking is of man, it will fail;
but if it is of God, you will not be able to overthrow them. You might
even be found opposing God!

Before identifying the two issues in Acts 5:35–37 it is important
to recognize our limitations as modern readers of texts like these.
Unlike the discipline of modern history, where scholars are over-
whelmed with the sheer quantity of source material, it is the opposite
for those who study the world of antiquity, where only a fraction
of documents and artefacts have survived the ravages of the ages.
Humility is appropriate in addressing the problems in this passage,
but also gratitude that we have this passage at all.

There are two problems and the first is more easily explained than
the second.[6]

The first problem is that Gamaliel said, 'before these days
Theudas rose up' and that '*after* him Judas the Galilean rose up'. This
is in apparent conflict with Josephus, who states that Theudas led
his insurrection in the mid-40s, *thirty years after* the uprising of Judas
the Galilean (Josephus, *Ant.* 18.3; 20.97–99).

There is no record of a Theudas who arose before Judas' uprising
in AD 6–7. However, Theudas is an abbreviation of Theodotus (gift
of God), which in turn is the Greek version of the Hebrew name
Jonathan. Was Gamaliel referring to another otherwise unknown
insurrectionist named Theudas who arose during the time of
Archelaus (3 BC – AD 6) or, before him, of Herod (40–4 BC)?

Whilst this is theoretically possible, it is unlikely because Gamaliel's
quoted words about Theudas and Judas closely match Josephus'

---

6. See further F. F. Bruce, *Commentary on the Book of Acts* (Edinburgh:
Marshall, Morgan & Scott, 1956), p. 125, n. 47; R. Riesner, *Paul's Early
Period* (Grand Rapids: Eerdmans, 1998), pp. 330–332.

references to men of that name. However, Josephus wrote his *Jewish Antiquities* in the mid-90s, well after Luke wrote Luke-Acts, so Luke could not have derived his information from that source. On the face of it Luke has made an understandable mistake. Luke, or the source he depended on, had merely mixed up the sequence by wrongly placing Theudas before Judas. This is not a major blemish on Luke's qualities as a historian of the period.

The other problem, however, is not so readily explained. It is that the Theudas incident occurred while Cuspius Fadus was procurator of Judea in AD 46–48, whereas Luke quotes Gamaliel's speaking to the Sanhedrin about him around twelve years earlier!

There are several possible explanations for these issues. The first is to lay a double accusation at the feet of Luke, that he has muddled the Judas–Theudas sequence and, more seriously, that he has anachronistically put words into the mouth of Gamaliel.

The second possible explanation is that the fault lies with the source or sources Luke used. In favour of this is the fact that for all events prior to those in which he was personally involved Luke depended on hearsay or written fragmentary chronicles. It is one thing to accuse Luke of errors in details of events of people contemporary with him, but it is another to do so where he would have been entirely dependent on what he had been told about the Gamaliel incident or upon an earlier written account of that incident.

Problems in perspective

Honesty demands recognition of problems with two of Luke's texts, Luke 2:2 and Acts 5:35–37. Nonetheless, as I have suggested, there are mitigating circumstances with both texts. The apparent error in Luke 2:2 may be due to something as simple as an ungrammatical lapse, and the errors in Acts 5:35–37 are perhaps due to mistakes in the written or oral sources on which Luke depended. It is reasonable to excuse a historian in antiquity for replicating errors in the sources available to him. Today we are able to check historical information in a matter of seconds by a few clicks on our keyboards, but written encyclopedias, archives and public records would not have been available for Luke.

On the other hand, however, even if we were to concede that problems are to be found in these two texts, would that condemn Luke's work overall? My argument is that Luke and the other writers in the New Testament allow us to see a 'big picture' of the rise and spread of Christianity from the mid-30s to the mid-90s that occurred at the impulse of the man Jesus, his life, teachings, death and resurrection. It is simply a wrong procedure to magnify difficulties in two problematic texts and pronounce negatively on the origins of Christianity, which is so amply chronicled in the great majority of unproblematic texts.

Events and people contemporary with Luke

It is obvious that we must distinguish between information Luke received from others – whether written or oral – and those people and events he personally encountered. The latter fall into two categories, well-known people and less well-known people.

Amongst famous people we meet in the Acts of the Apostles are Sergius Paulus, the Roman proconsul of Cyprus (Acts 13:7–12), the Roman procurators of Judea, Felix (with Drusilla) and Festus (Acts 24:24, 27), King Agrippa II, with his sister Bernice (Acts 25:13), and Publius, chief man of Malta (Acts 27:7).

We also meet less famous yet significant people such as Antipas' courtier Manaen in Antioch (13:1), Elymas the magician in Cyprus (13:8), Dionysius the Areopagite in Athens (17:34), Demetrius the silversmith in Ephesus (19:24), the tribune Claudius Lysias in Jerusalem (23:26), the advocate Tertullus in Caesarea (24:1–2) and the centurion Julius in Paul's journey to Rome (27:1). This list of public figures, some major some minor, is impressive and not reasonably doubted.

Since Luke proves to be accurate with well-known persons and events, we may reasonably express confidence in his references to lesser persons about whom the major historical sources make no mention. References to these public figures, some major, some minor, is compelling and not reasonably doubted.

The trivia of Acts

Much of Paul's work, as recorded in Acts, occurred in the Roman provinces of Cyprus, Galatia, Asia, Macedonia and Achaia. After they conquered a region, the Romans wisely allowed local methods of government to continue for a period before imposing a uniform Roman bureaucracy. Writing of the era in which Acts describes Paul's labours in the 50s, the noted Roman historian Edwin Judge comments, 'The standardization of government had by no means worked itself out, nor was Roman control yet evenly imposed in every quarter. The Acts of the Apostles is a kaleidoscope of local diversity.'[7]

The eminent Roman historian A. N. Sherwin-White has examined incidental references in the Acts to trials, punishment, city government and citizenship. In case after case he finds that the 'narrative agrees with the evidence of the earlier period', that is, the era of the apostles (AD 30–70). In summary, Sherwin-White states about the Acts, 'Any attempt to reject its basic historicity even in matters of detail must now appear absurd.'[8]

Acts indeed captures the sense of local diversity referred to above, as these examples indicate. In Thessalonica the decisions about Paul were made by 'the politarchs' (Acts 17:8), a word that appears rarely in ancient books. The inscription over the archway

---

7. E. A. Judge, 'The Decrees of Caesar at Thessalonica', *RTR* 30.1 (1971), p. 7.
8. A. N. Sherwin-White, *Roman Society and Roman Law in the New Testament* (Oxford: Oxford University Press, 1965), p. 189.

of the Vandar Gate at Thessalonica, now in the British Museum, reads, 'In the time of the politarchs . . . ', thus demonstrating Luke's accuracy.

Similarly, in the account of the riot in Ephesus, capital of Asia, Luke refers to 'the Asiarchs' who begged Paul not to enter the theatre (Acts 19:31). Strabo, who wrote about the geography of the times, referred to 'the Asiarchs . . . the first men of their province' (*Geogr.* 14.1.42).

Finally, on the island of Malta Luke's reference to 'the chief man of the island, named Publius' (Acts 28:7) is confirmed by an inscription which refers to another person who held that office ('Pudens, equite of the Romans, chief man of Malta'[9]). Space prevents the citation of more evidence, but enough has been presented to make the point that Luke carefully preserves the detailed accuracy of local customs of government.

The verdicts of ancient historians on Luke

Curiously many New Testament scholars pass a negative verdict on Luke as a historian, for example, E. Haenchen: 'Luke was no professional historian and he was not interested in writing a history of early Christianity . . . ' Rather, he declares, 'the book of Acts gives rich history about . . . "the post-apostolic age"'.[10] In other words, Luke-Acts is useful for insights into the period when it was written (the 80s and 90s according to liberal scholars), but relatively worthless for the period it narrated (i.e. 6 BC – AD 62).

By contrast, many eminent classicists and ancient historians write positively about Luke. The reason is that historians of the classical world understand the uneven nature of the sources available to them, which they do not approach with unrealistic expectations.

---

9. *IG* 14.601.

10. Quoted C. Hemer, *The Book of Acts in the Setting of Hellenistic History* (Tübingen: Mohr, 1989), p. 101, n. 7.

In regard to historiography the noted German scholar Theodore Mommsen observed about the Acts of the Apostles, 'the numerous small features – features not really necessary for the actual course of the action and yet which fit so well there – are internal witnesses to his reliability'.[11]

Eduard Meyer, another distinguished historian of classical antiquity, commented that Luke's work, in spite of a more limited content, 'bears the same character as those of great historians, of a Polybius, a Livy and many others'.[12] Meyer, who was critical of Christianity, wrote:

> for the history of Christianity . . . we have the completely inestimable
> advantage . . . of having access to the portrayal of the beginning stages
> of the development directly from the pen of one of its co-participants.
> That alone ensures for the author an eminent place among the significant
> historians of world history.[13]

More recently Martin Hengel pointed out that the book of Acts 'always remains within the limits of what was considered reliable by the standards of antiquity'.[14]

Classical scholar and traveller in Asia Minor Colin Hemer for many years engaged in painstaking study of what he calls the 'trivia of Acts' in place names, topographical and travel details and titles of local officials. After exhaustive tabulation of such detail Hemer, a model of caution, notes that he had 'discovered a wealth of material suggesting an author familiar with particular locations and at the times in question'. After examining these details Hemer concluded that 'By and large these all converged to support the

---

11. Quoted R. Riesner, *Paul's Early Years* (ET Grand Rapids: Eerdmans, 1998), p. 326.

12. Quoted Bruce, *Acts*, p. 27.

13. Quoted Riesner, *Paul's Early Years*, p. 326.

14. M. Hengel, *Acts and the History of Earliest Christianity* (ET London: SCM, 1979), p. 61.

general reliability of the narrative, through details so intricately yet often unintentionally woven into that narrative.'[15]

The assumption of some New Testament scholars that the author of Luke-Acts was concerned only about matters relating to theology and not history must be questioned. In the light of Luke's historical interest and competence noted above by famous ancient historians we are able with confidence, tempered with critical caution, to make use of his texts to understand the birth and growth of earliest Christianity. At the same time we must not force him and other New Testament writers to use the techniques and standards of modern historiography. Such expectations are unreasonable and impractical.

Yet New Atheists appear to approach the New Testament and its connections with the world of its time with precisely unreasonable expectations. They find fault with several texts without sympathetic understanding of the limitations of those texts and then make wholesale negative conclusions about the overall historicity of the New Testament. The better approach is to accept that, globally speaking, the story of the New Testament from Bethlehem to Patmos is coherent and reasonable.

It must be remembered that ancient-history studies are not mathematically precise in the same way, for example, as physics is. Yet atheists seem to demand that precision, and when they do not find it throw up their arms and declare the history of the New Testament to be full of errors. The argument of this chapter is that the reverse is true, that we find here a narrative that is overall credible and that is only reasonably explained by the historical impact of a massive figure such as Jesus.

---

15. Hemer, *Acts*, p. 412.

6. ARCHAEOLOGY AND ARTEFACTS

The results of archaeological excavations help to constrain the imaginations of scholars who would mythologize the New Testament.
John McRay, archaeologist

The discovery of artefacts relating to the New Testament began in the 1800s and continues to this day. Sometimes discoveries were made in the course of deliberate excavations, but at other times they were made accidentally in the course of road works and similar routine activities in Jerusalem and elsewhere.[1]

Usually these artefacts are stones with words inscribed on them. A manuscript like P[52], a fragment of John 18 dating from early in the second century, is also an artefact, but because it is not the original text we regard it as a 'secondary' artefact. By contrast, a stone with an inscription from the era of the New Testament is a 'primary' artefact. Discovery of such artefacts has proved exciting,

---

1. See J. Rousseau and R. Arav, *Jesus and His World* (Minneapolis: Fortress, 1995); J. Finegan, *The Archeology of the New Testament: The Life of Jesus and the Beginning of the Early Church* (Princeton: Princeton University Press, 1969); *The Archeology of the New Testament: The Mediterranean World of the Early Christian Apostles* (Boulder: Westview, 1981); J. McRay, *Archaeology of the New Testament* (Grand Rapids: Baker, 1991).

but also frequently quite illuminating since they often help us confirm the veracity of the New Testament story as well as understand better the texts of the New Testament.

Jesus in Galilee

Sepphoris (near Nazareth) and Tiberias (on the western side of the Lake) were the major cities of Galilee in the time of Jesus. Tiberias has been excavated only to a limited degree but it is otherwise with Sepphoris, which is only a few kilometres from Nazareth, Jesus' village. Josephus refers to both cities and the modern excavations complement our knowledge from the written text. However, the information from Sepphoris and Tiberias is not especially relevant to Jesus since he seems to have avoided these major settlements and their elite leaders, preferring to frequent the smaller towns and villages.

It is particularly significant, therefore, that archaeologists have unearthed as much as they have of Capernaum, the town Jesus used as his base in Galilee. It was a settlement of between 600 and 1,500 inhabitants that nestled behind a sea wall and simple breakwaters. The village consisted of single-storey stone *insulae*, apartments with internal courtyards shared by several families. The large white limestone synagogue from later centuries was probably built on the existing black basalt foundations of the earlier synagogue where Jesus preached. The extensive remains of houses in Capernaum give us a good sense of how Jesus and his first disciples lived in Capernaum.

Capernaum was a short distance from the Via Maris highway that linked Egypt with Mesopotamia, along which a succession of travellers passed. As well, Capernaum with Chorazin and Bethsaida formed a triangle of Jewish villages in whose synagogues Jesus taught. Moreover, Capernaum was conveniently close to the border of Gaulanitis to provide Jesus with a way of escape from the suspicious tetrarch, Herod Antipas, who lived in Tiberias a few kilometres down the lakeside.

In 1985 near Ginosar (Gennesaret, Mark 6:53) in Galilee an ancient fishing boat was discovered and later painstakingly restored. Scholars believe it came from the era of Jesus and was preserved under water during the intervening years. It was a large boat that could accommodate six or seven fishermen. In the museum in the kibbutz En Gev across the lake are stone anchors and weights for nets, giving us good reason to believe the Gospel narratives about fishing and fishermen on the lake. The name of the village Magdala (Migdal) means a 'tower' for spotting fish. It was the home of Mary of Magdala, a woman 'of means' who with other local women provided financially for Jesus and the disciples (Luke 8:3). Josephus refers to Migdal by another name, Taricheae, which means 'dried fish'.

In a dispute with scribes from Jerusalem who had come to Galilee, Jesus refers to the practice of dedicating money to God that should have been used to care for one's elderly parents (Mark 7:11). Jesus referred to such dedicated money as 'Corban', which is corroborated by the words on an ossuary (bone chest) discovered in Jerusalem in 1956: 'Everything that a man will find to his profit in this ossuary is an offering (*qorban*) to God from the one within it.'[2]

Jesus in Samaria

According to John's narrative, Jesus came to Sychar in Samaria, 'near the field that Jacob gave to his son Joseph. Jacob's [deep] well was there ... the woman [of Samaria] said to him ... "Our fathers worshipped on this mountain..."' (John 4:5, 11, 19–20). These details (Joseph's field, Jacob's well, this mountain) coordinate with the deep well that is close to the traditional site of Joseph's tomb, which in turn is near Mount Gerizim, the cult centre of the Samaritan religion. The Talmud refers to a spring called Ain Soker, which resembles John's 'Sychar'.[3] John's remark that 'Jews have no dealings

2. C. A. Evans, 'Jesus and the Ossuaries', *BBR* 13.1 (2003), pp. 21–46.
3. F. F. Bruce, *Places They Knew* (London: Ark, 1981), pp. 35–38.

with Samaritans' (John 4:9) more literally means, 'Jews will not *eat together with* Samaritans.' This was because Jews regarded Samaritans as irretrievably 'unclean' ('daughters of the Samaritans are menstruants from their cradle', *m. Nid.* 4.1).

Jesus in the far north

Following the feeding of the multitude when the people attempted to force kingship on him (John 6:15), Jesus travelled outside Herod Antipas' jurisdiction through the principalities of Tyre and Sidon to the cities of the Decapolis (Mark 7:24, 31). Along the way he went to Caesarea Philippi, capital of the tetrarchy of Herod Philip. At that time the Jordan River flowed out of the Grotto of Pan adjoining the temple of Pan, god of remote places, the remains of which are still to be seen (cf. Josephus, *War* 1.104–105). Mark correctly refers to the 'villages of Caesarea Philippi' (Mark 8:27), satellites of this northern city that sits on the slopes of Mount Hermon.

Jesus in Jerusalem

In 1964 a succession of digs from the previous century finally established the extensive pool complex in the grounds of St Anne's Church, Jerusalem. Many had believed that the Pool of Bethesda was an invention of John (John 5:1–9). This archaeological discovery confirms that the description of this pool was not the creation of John but reflects an accurate and detailed knowledge of the site. The Gospel gives (1) the name of the pool as Bethesda, (2) its location near the Sheep Gate, and (3) the fact that it has five porticos with rushing water. All these details have been corroborated through literary and archaeological evidence, affirming the historical accuracy of John's account.

Discoveries continue to be made. In 2005 the Pool of Siloam was uncovered on the southern slopes of the old City of David. It was

fed by water from the tunnel of Hezekiah that came from the Gihon
Spring and had been used in Jesus' day for ritual purification. Water
from this pool was taken in procession by priests and poured out in
the temple during the Feast of Tabernacles (*m. Suk.* 4.9: '[The priests]
filled a golden flagon holding a litre of water from Siloam. When
they reached the water gate they blew the shofar . . . '[4]). The discovery
of this pool confirms the narrative of John 9.

In 1941 in the Kidron area of Jerusalem an ossuary was discovered bearing the name 'Alexander the Cyrene, son of Simon'.[5] It
is too much a coincidence that Mark 15:21 states, 'they compelled a
passer-by, *Simon* of Cyrene . . . the father of *Alexander* . . . to carry
his cross . . . ' The words on the ossuary appear to coincide with
Mark's reference.

Also dramatic was the discovery in Jerusalem in 1990 of an
ossuary bearing the name *Yehoseph bar Qyph*, Joseph Caiaphas.[6]
Josephus also mentions Caiaphas, but it is only from the New
Testament that we know he was the son-in-law of the senior high
priest, Annas (John 18:13). The New Testament provides information not found in other sources. In this artefact we now have
'hard evidence' relating to those who were responsible for the
crucifixion of Jesus.

In 1961 in Caesarea Maritima Italian archaeologists found an
inscription bearing the name 'Pontius Pilate, Prefect of Judea' that
was apparently attached to a 'Tiberium', a building dedicated to
Tiberius Caesar.[7] Although a relatively minor governor, Pilate is
referred to in Josephus, Philo and Tacitus, as well as in the Gospels
and book of Acts. But in this discovery we now have an artefact
made under the instructions of this man. This inscription settles the
question of Pilate's title. He was 'prefect of Judea', the *military* (not
civilian) governor.

---

4. H. Danby, *The Mishnah* (Oxford: Clarendon, 1972).

5. Evans, 'Jesus and the Ossuaries', pp. 21–46.

6. Ibid.

7. Ibid.

Also dramatic was the discovery near Jerusalem in 1968 of the remains of the man Yehohanan, who had been crucified in the first century and who had been nailed through his feet to the cross.[8] Yehohanan's lower leg was fractured. This may support John 19:31–35, where it was proposed that Jesus' legs should be broken. Yehohanan was buried in a family grave, tending to validate Jesus' burial in a similar family tomb and not in a common pit appropriate to felons, as some maintain in denial of Jesus' burial in a known tomb.

The early church in Jerusalem

In 1913 a substantial dedication was found in Jerusalem relating to a Greek-speaking synagogue that also provided hostel accommodation for foreign Jews.[9] Theodotus, a priest and synagogue leader, dedicated this synagogue 'for the reading of the Law and the teaching of the commandments'. This inscription, significantly written in Greek, confirms Acts 6:5, 9, which refers to various synagogues for 'Hellenist' (Greek-speaking) Jews from the Diaspora living in Jerusalem.

Caesarea Maritima

The central coastline of Palestine lacks a natural harbour, so in 25–13 BC Herod created an artificial harbour at a place called Straton's Tower. Herod's engineers built two massive breakwaters to enclose a harbour of 100,000 square metres. Herod built a palace in Caesarea and a large hippodrome, whose remains are still to be seen. In recent times archaeologists have unearthed an inner harbour from which

---

8. Ibid.; Rousseau and Arav, *Jesus and His World*, pp. 74–78.
9. R. Riesner, 'Synagogues in Jerusalem', in R. Bauckham (ed.), *The Book of Acts in Its First Century Setting* (Grand Rapids: Eerdmans, 1995), vol. 4, pp. 192–200.

small boats went out to vessels within the harbour. From AD 6, when Augustus annexed Judea, Caesarea became the capital of the province. As noted above, Pilate dedicated a temple in Caesarea to Tiberius in Caesarea. Peter came to Caesarea to preach to the household of the centurion Cornelius (Acts 10:24). King Agrippa I, who had James Zebedee killed and Peter arrested, was struck down in the theatre in Caesarea (Acts 12:21–23). It was from Caesarea that Paul departed several times by ship, including his journey to Rome for trial before Caesar following his two years of imprisonment in Caesarea (Acts 9:30; 18:22; 27:1).

Cyprus and Antioch in Pisidia

In the Island of Cyprus, which was a Roman province, Paul was responsible for the conversion of the proconsul, Sergius Paulus (Acts 13:7–12). A boundary stone in Rome mentioning 'Sergius' was discovered in 1887. It records the appointment in AD 47 of a Sergius as a curator of the banks of the Tiber. It is possible that Sergius first served his three years as proconsul at Cyprus, then returned to Rome, where he was appointed curator.

Be that as it may, after Cyprus Paul travelled directly through the Taurus Mountains to Antioch in Pisidia (modern Yalvaç). In that city a stone bearing the names of the Paulli family has been discovered, suggesting that Paul deliberately came to a city where relatives of the Proconsul of Cyprus lived, who may have provided for Paul and Barnabas. Patronage and support, including from non-believers, were important to a vulnerable missionary like Paul (see e.g. Acts 19:31, 'some of the *Asiarchs*, who were friends of [Paul] . . . were urging him not to venture into the theatre'[10]).

Sir William Ramsay was amongst the succession of archaeologists who excavated Antioch of Pisidia, which is the hub of a network

---

10. Asiarchs were members of the Supreme Council of the province of Roman Asia and were of necessity cult priests in the temples.

of Roman roads. It is surely no coincidence that Saul became known as Paul in and after his time in Cyprus, through his connection with Sergius *Paulus* (Acts 13:9).

Other cities of Paul and John

In the later 1800s an inscription was discovered in Thessalonica bearing the words 'In the time of the Politarchs',[11] confirming Acts 17:6, 'They dragged Jason and some of the brothers before the city authorities [Politarchs].' This word, meaning 'first men of the city', was a title used locally. Within a few decades the Romans would have imposed their own bureaucratic titles for local officials. The reference in Acts 17:6 is consistent with Paul's travels in the middle of the first century.

Also in the late 1800s a pavement in Corinth was unearthed with the words 'Erastus, commissioner for public works', which may refer to the Erastus Paul mentions in Romans 16:23 ('Erastus, the city treasurer . . . [greets] you'). Recovered also in Corinth is the stone with the words 'SYNAGOGUE OF THE HEBREWS', which is consistent with Paul's preaching in the synagogue in Corinth (though the dating of the inscription is uncertain).

In the late 1800s an inscription at Delphi was found bearing the name of the newly appointed proconsul, Gallio: '[C]laudius . . . year 12 acclaimed emperor for the 26th time [i.e. AD 52] . . . I have long been zealous for the city of Delphi . . . those quarrels of which report has been made by Lucius Junius Gallio my friend and proconsul of Achaia.'

This suggests that Gallio had been appointed in AD 51, which in turn casts important light on Acts 18:12 ('when Gallio was proconsul of Achaia'), pinpointing Paul's probable arrival in the Achaian capital in AD 50. This in turn dovetails with Acts 18:2, where Aquila and Priscilla arrived in Corinth having been expelled with other Jews

---

11. G. H. R. Horsley, 'Politarchs', *ABD* 5, pp. 384–389.

from Italy, which appears to have occurred in AD 49 (Suetonius, *Claud.* 25.4: 'Since the Jews constantly made disturbances at the instigation of Chrestus he expelled them from Rome'[12]).

Ephesus, near the west coast of Roman Asia was the city where Paul spent three years preaching the message of Christ. The silversmiths' guild instigated a riot against Paul because he preached against the patron deity Artemis, whose vast temple was in Ephesus. The people of Ephesus, calling for the death of Paul, gathered in the great theatre. The remains of effigies of Artemis are exhibited in the museum in Selçuk near Ephesus. The great theatre that accommodated 25,000 people continues to attract thousands of visitors to ancient Ephesus.

Ephesus was also the centre of ministry to the apostle John. Remains of the Temple of Domitian dominated the ancient city and part of the great statue of this Caesar, whom Revelation calls 'the Beast', are exhibited in the Selçuk museum near the ancient city.

The other cities John addresses were Smyrna, Pergamum, Thyatira, Sardis, Philadelphia and Laodicea. Modern development has obscured the ancient cities of Smyrna, Thyatira and Philadelphia but much of Pergamum, Sardis and Laodicea have been excavated, revealing Greco-Roman cities of great wealth and beauty. Many of the details about the message to the church in Laodicea fit very well with information about that great city from those times, for example,

---

12. J. C. Rolphe, LCL (Cambridge, Mass.: Heinemann, 1914). According to Dio Cassius, in AD 41 Claudius 'did not drive them out' but forbade the Jews 'to hold meetings' (*Hist. Rom.* 60.6.6), whereas according to Suetonius he 'expelled the Jews from Rome' (*Claud.* 25.4). The two actions are to be distinguished. We depend on Orosius for dating the expulsion to AD 49, a date some doubt; e.g. J. Murphy-O'Connor, *St Paul's Corinth* (Wilmington: Michael Glazier, 1983), pp. 130–132, who points out that Orosius depends on information for this dating on Josephus who, however, is silent on this. However, the conjunction of Aquila's and Priscilla's *uncertain* arrival date and Gallio's *known* arrival date makes it likely that the two arrivals occurred within a year or two of each other and that Paul's arrival in Corinth occurred in between, that is, in AD 50.

the lukewarm water (between the hot springs of Hierapolis and the icy water from the Honaz mountains near Colosse), the wealth of the city (its gold and fine wool) and its medical reputation for eye salve.

Paul's final visit to Jerusalem

In 1871 the warning against a Gentile's entering the temple precincts on pain of death was discovered, confirming Acts 21:28 where the complaint against Paul was that he had brought Greeks into the temple.[13]

Conclusion

Some of these archaeological discoveries are relatively minor, whilst others are spectacular. Taken together they both elucidate and indirectly confirm the historical narratives in the New Testament. For example, there are numerous coins from the era bearing names of Herod, his sons Archelaus and Antipas, his grandson Herod Agrippa I and his great-grandson Herod Agrippa II. Furthermore there are extant statues of the Roman Caesars of the era – Augustus, Tiberius, Gaius ('Caligula'), Claudius, Nero, Vespasian, Titus and Domitian. Again, excavations in Jerusalem, Gamla, Masada, Sepphoris, Tiberias, Capernaum, Chorazin in Israel convey useful information about houses and synagogues of the era. Restorations in cities such as Ephesus give an idea of public spaces, houses, furniture, tools, medical implements, public administration, and so on, which enlarges our understanding of Paul's ministry in Greco-Roman cities. Furthermore I have not even referred to the Qumran scrolls, discovered in 1947, which attest the existence, beliefs and practices of the Essenes, a Jewish sect active in the time of Jesus.

---

13. Evans, 'Jesus and the Ossuaries', pp. 21–46.

Much more could be written on the subject of the archaeology of the New Testament. What I have written here is a mere outline. But the material in this chapter is sufficient to illustrate the point that New Testament history from Bethlehem to Patmos is a true history confirmed at many points by archaeological discoveries.

7. GOSPEL TRUTH AND CONTRADICTIONS

The Gospels are a sub-type of Greco-Roman biography.
David Aune

The New Atheists chiefly depend on the argument that the gospel writers contradict themselves. Whilst they make a priority of the (alleged) contradictions in the infancy narratives (see chapter 8), they also point to other 'contradictions' in the Gospels. According to Hitchens, the authors of the Gospels cannot 'agree on anything of importance'.[1] The internal inconsistencies within the Gospels confirm to the New Atheists that they are unreliable as historical records and therefore do not have any 'divine' origin or authority.

Reality check

Before addressing this issue it is important to recognize several realities about the Gospels. First, as ancient records they share the

---

1. Hitchens, *God Is Not Great: How Religion Poisons Everything* (New York: Twelve, 2007), p. 111.

limitations of other texts of their times. Their authors wrote by hand on cumbersome scrolls, with no opportunity to make corrections as they went. A slip of the pen usually meant rewriting the scroll from the beginning. Except for the very wealthy, ordinary people had no access to the writings of others, so the resources for research we take for granted were simply not available. This meant there was no easy way of cross-checking information.

Secondly, we need to ask why there was not one Gospel but multiple Gospels? This question is quite pointed because it is generally agreed that two writers (Matthew and Luke) had an earlier text (Mark) in front of them, and that a fourth writer (John) at least knew of these other texts. If three of the authors knew of the existence of another Gospel why did they need to write yet another? That they did can mean only one thing: each of the four had a distinctive perspective on Jesus and a distinctive audience that impelled him to write *his* Gospel for that audience. Each 'saw' Jesus through his own eyes and each was writing about him for *his* audience.

One striking thing about Matthew and Luke is that they do not criticize their primary narrative source, Mark. On the contrary, their incorporation of Mark into their own narratives speaks volumes of their high opinion of his Gospel. This is not because authors then passively and uncritically accepted the works of others. In fact, the opposite is true. Historians and biographers were quick to contradict and criticize the blemishes in the works of others. For example, Josephus devoted his book *Against Apion* to demolishing the work of a historian who had criticized Josephus' history of the Jewish people in his multi-volume *Jewish Antiquities*. There are numerous examples of historians criticizing historians, but Matthew and Luke in no way criticize or contradict Mark.[2] On the contrary,

---

2. See P. T. Massey, 'Disagreement in the Greco-Roman Literary Tradition and the Implications for Gospel Research', *BBR* 22.1 (2012), pp. 51–80, who observes, 'in comparison to Greco-Roman convention, direct disagreement does not characterize the fourfold gospel' (p. 78).

they endorse their predecessor as they supplement and amplify his briefer text from other sources.

The Gospels are not photographs so much as impressionistic portrayals that idiosyncratically presented Jesus for people of differing backgrounds and ethnicities. Inevitably each writer brings out differing aspects about Jesus and selects and uses material at his disposal accordingly. Thus it needs to be recognized that each Gospel is a *literary* work (crafted for a particular use) whilst at the same time being *biographical* (as to genre).

The New Atheists, however, demand that the Gospels fit their paradigm of perfection, and when they do not fulfil their criteria they pronounce them fatally flawed. Their heightened and unreasonable expectation predetermines their negative verdict. It is inappropriate, however, to demand standards of mathematical precision from texts in that era, or, for that matter, in any era. Historical texts are not scientific formulae.

'Contradictions' from silence: Mark and John

One of the striking characteristics of John's Gospel is that the author omits a number of key elements from Mark (and therefore also from Matthew and Luke).

- The temptations
- Jesus' public 'kingdom' proclamation in Galilee
- Harvest parables
- Exorcisms
- Table fellowship with 'sinners'
- Jesus' formal appointment of twelve disciples
- Peter's messianic confession at Caesarea Philippi
- The transfiguration of Jesus
- The institution of the Lord's Supper
- Jesus' Gethsemane prayer
- The Sanhedrin trial

The sceptical mind declares John's omissions to be contradictions. But does it follow that an omission is necessarily a contradiction? It is quite possible that Mark and John each included the material they did because it was *available* to them and they regarded it as important for *their* audiences.

Mark's and John's respective emphases in their Gospels give us a good idea of their intentions in writing for their audiences. Mark's purpose was to present the crucified but resurrected Jesus as the true 'Son of God' to non-Jewish readers in the Roman world, where the Caesar, as ruler of the world, was regarded as a divine figure (see Mark 1:1; 15:39). Mark sets his narrative mostly in Galilee.

By contrast, John was writing mainly for Jewish Christians whose faith was under challenge (John 20:31, 'these [things] are written so that you may [continue to] believe'). This explains why John sets his narrative mostly in Jerusalem at the time of the great feasts, in particular the Passover. John points to Jesus as the divine fulfilment but also the instrument for the *discontinuity* of those feasts (e.g. as the Lamb of God fulfilling the Feast of Passover, as water for the thirsty and light for the world, fulfilling the Feast of Tabernacles: John 1:29; 7:37; 8:12).

Mark and John are mindful of their readers' situation and shape their Gospels accordingly by including and excluding material they think necessary. Such differing objectives explain well the respective items Mark and John include or omit from their Gospels.

At the same time, a strong case can be made for the historical and geographical integrity of both Mark and John. Mark's Galilee-focused biography reflects the subtle tensions between the villages of Capernaum and Nazareth and the political realities that prompted Jesus' various withdrawals from Herod Antipas' jurisdiction, the tetrarchy of Galilee, whose capital was Tiberias.

Mark wrote his Gospel some years before AD 70, that is, within a generation of Jesus, so its details were subject to scrutiny by contemporaries of Jesus. Matthew and Luke independently valued Mark's biography so highly that they incorporated its outline, sequence and much of its content in their own biographies, often word for word.[3] Matthew reproduces 90% and Luke about 50% of Mark. But Matthew and Luke have other source material to weave into and around Mark's text.

John locates Jesus mainly in Jerusalem, where references to the pools of Bethesda and Siloam and the Portico of Solomon are consistent with the known streetscape of Herod's Jerusalem. This Gospel reflects the political situation of the era of Tiberius (AD 14–37), where the high priest in the temple city was able to exploit the vulnerability of the Roman prefect to his own advantage, such was the delicate balance then (but not later) between the secular and sacred power.

Moreover, the 'disciple whom Jesus loved' would have known about the incidents in Mark's book that, for his own reasons, he omits. It is likely also that his readers knew of these incidents (John 21:20, 24). This is not to say that John had Mark's Gospel in front of him when he came to write his Gospel, as Matthew and Luke did. Almost certainly John wrote independently of Mark. Yet he would have known of the existence of Mark and the kinds of details he included.

'Contradictions' from silence: Josephus and Philo

The so-called 'contradictions from silence' find interesting parallels in Josephus and Philo, Jewish writers from the first century. Both historians record the same event: Caligula's planned attack on the Jewish temple in AD 40.[4] Philo mentions the prelude to the episode, the Jews' destruction of a statue of the emperor in Jamnia

---

3. C. S. Keener, 'Otho: A Targeted Comparison of Suetonius' Biography and Tacitus' History, with Implications for the Gospels' Reliability', *BBR* 21.3 (2011), pp. 331–356.

4. E. M. Smallwood, 'Philo and Josephus as Historians of the Same Events', in L. H. Feldman and G. Hata (eds.), *Josephus, Judaism, and Christianity* (Leiden: Brill, 1987), pp. 114–132.

(*Legat.* 200–203) and also Governor Petronius' summons of Jewish leaders to explain and accept Caligula's intentions (*Legat.* 221–224). For his part and for whatever reason, however, Josephus is silent about these details. Yet Josephus' silence does not necessarily contradict Philo's account. He may not have had access to the information or alternatively did not consider it important enough to include.

Another example is found in the accounts of the Gospel of Mark and Josephus regarding John the Baptist (Mark 1:2–8; 6:14–29; *Ant.* 18.116–119). Josephus refers to John's baptizing but does not mention the Jordan River, as Mark does. Josephus attributes John's arrest to Antipas' jealousy of John's popularity, whereas Mark gives the reason as John's criticism for the tetrarch's marriage to the wife of a brother who was still alive. Mark describes John's death in the setting of the birthday of Herod Antipas, but Josephus is silent about this. Josephus gives the place of John's execution as Machaerus, but Mark does not indicate the location.

Are these silences contradictions? Not necessarily. It is almost certain that John baptized in the Jordan. The motives for John's arrest – jealousy and anger – are most likely complementary and are credible. Machaerus, an isolated fortress established by Herod the king in Perea, was a suitable place to imprison John, a popular prophet with numerous supporters. The setting of John's death in a drunken banquet is likewise believable. Accordingly it is reasonable to combine the details from these independent sources to form an overall understanding about John the Baptist. An omission is not necessarily an error.

The global agreement of Mark and John

Any discussion of the omissions from these Gospels must be done with an understanding of Mark's and John's differing intentions and audiences. Moreover the wealth of their respective historical, cultural and geographical detail points to their respective integrity as biographers of Jesus. To these must be added their agreement as to the overall sequence of Jesus' ministry.

In spite of the omissions from each other (as above) there is broad agreement between Mark and John about the overall sequence of events concerning Jesus (see table 7.1 below).

Table 7.1 The public ministry of Jesus of Nazareth

	Mark	*John*
John's baptizing in the Jordan	1:4–8	1:31; 4:26
John baptizes Jesus	1:9–11	1:33
Jesus calls disciples	1:16–20	1:35–51
Arrest of John	1:14	3:24
Jesus in Galilee	1:14 – 7:23	2:12; 4:46–54; 7:1
Feeding of 5,000	6:30–44	6:1–13
Triumphal entry into Jerusalem	11:1–10	12:12–19
Jewish trial of Jesus	14:53–55	18:12–14, 19–24
Roman trial of Jesus	15:1–5	18:28 – 19:16
Crucifixion of Jesus and two others	15:24–32	19:17–18
Burial of Jesus in Joseph's tomb	15:42–47	19:38–42
Discovery of empty tomb on Sunday	16:1–8	20:1–10
Resurrection appearances	16:7[5]	20:11 – 21:14

The occurrence of these events *in the same sequence* is significant and must be kept in mind to maintain a sense of historical perspective.[6] Both Mark and John begin with John's baptisms (including of Jesus) and end with the empty tomb and the resurrection appearances.

---

5. Implicit in Mark 16:7, where the angel says to the women, 'Go, tell his disciples and Peter that he is going before you to Galilee. There you will see him, just as he told you.'

6. So J. D. G. Dunn, 'John and the Oral Gospel Tradition', in H. Wansbrough (ed.), *Jesus and the Oral Gospel Tradition*, JSNTSup 64 (Sheffield: JSOT, 1991), pp. 351–379.

'Contradictions' of fact: Mark and John

There are two apparent contradictions between Mark and John, both
regarding matters of sequence: the clearing of the temple and the
Last Supper.

The clearing of the temple

Mark (11:15–18), followed by Matthew and Luke, locates the temple
clearing in Jesus' final week in Jerusalem as the major reason for his
arrest and ultimate crucifixion. It can scarcely be doubted that Jesus
expelled the merchants at that time.

John, however, places the clearing of the temple at the beginning
of Jesus' ministry (John 2:13–23).

Perhaps, though, John deliberately placed the event at the
beginning of his Gospel to allow space for his lengthy farewell dis-
courses at the end (chs. 13–17)? Or has he made a historical mistake?
For whatever reason, many authorities believe John has located the
event incorrectly, historically speaking.

For several reasons we should not lightly reach this conclusion.
First, a close comparison between John's and Mark's versions makes
it clear that neither author has depended on the other. True, in both
accounts Jesus cast out the moneychangers and overturned their
tables. Those actions, however, are implicit in any account of a
temple clearing. John's account is more vivid and detailed, referring
to oxen and sheep that Jesus drove out, his whip of cords and the
pouring out of the coins. The proposal that John had merely
adapted Mark's account and relocated it is not sustainable. It appears
that Mark and John have written up independent oral tradition
streams that are sufficiently distinctive to be describing two separate
events.

Secondly, John's account belongs to a series of events that
occurred *before* the arrest of John the Baptist (3:24), which belong
to the very early period of Jesus' ministry when he was still under
the shadow of John. According to Mark's account, however, Jesus
became a truly public figure only *after* the imprisonment of John the

Baptist. John's account tells us that Jesus was active for a period *prior* to John's arrest. It is readily imaginable that Jesus cleared the temple at that 'early' time when he was relatively unknown, perhaps in a less expansive manner than the dramatic and very public clearing at the end as described by Mark.

Thirdly, Malachi 3:1 ('I send my messenger, and he will prepare the way before me. And the Lord ... will suddenly come to his temple') closely connects the appearance of God's 'messenger' (John the Baptist) and the coming of the 'Lord' (the Messiah) to his temple. It can be argued that quite soon after John appeared in the wilderness Jesus deliberately came (as Lord) to the temple to fulfil Malachi's prophecy.

Fourthly, the Jews' observation 'It has taken forty-six years to build this temple' (John 2:20) has provoked much debate. One likely meaning is that the practical completion of the temple from its commencement in 20 BC took forty-six years, that is, until AD 26/27.[7] This fits in with the probable date of Jesus' baptism as AD 29/30 a year or so after the beginning of the preaching and baptizing of John the Baptist in Tiberius' fifteenth year, that is, AD 28/29 (see Luke 3:1–2). According to John's account, Jesus' clearing of the temple occurred soon after Jesus' baptism, during his first subsequent visit to Jerusalem. If the practices of the temple authorities were corrupt at the beginning of Jesus' ministry, they doubtless remained corrupt at the end of Jesus' ministry, when Mark records Jesus' clearing the traders from the sacred precinct.

In sum, it is entirely possible that Jesus 'cleansed' the temple *twice*, once at the beginning of his ministry and again at the end. The first may have been a little-noticed event, but the second was very public.

---

7. According to Josephus, *Ant.* 15.390, Herod commenced building the temple in 20 BC. In fact, work on the temple continued until AD 63 (*Ant.* 20.219). See H. Hoehner, *Chronological Aspects of the Life of Christ* (Grand Rapids: Zondervan, 1979), pp. 45–63.

The Last Supper

The Thursday evening meal in John 13:2 was not the Passover because that would be celebrated the next evening (Friday) after the lambs were sacrificed earlier *that* day (John 18:28; 19:14). What then of Mark 14:12, 16, where the meal on the same night (Thursday) was specifically called Passover? Are Mark and John contradicting one another?

The most likely explanations are that the Thursday night meal was either an *unofficial* early Passover or that the Galileans were following a *different* calendar from the official Jerusalem calendar. The high priest in Jerusalem followed the lunar calendar and the Qumran sect followed the solar calendar, so that key feasts fell on different dates in Jerusalem and Qumran.

Much of the Gospel of John is set in Passover contexts (2:13; [5:1?]; 6:4; 12:1 – 19:37). Near the beginning, John the Baptist hails Jesus as the *Lamb* of God who takes away the sin of the world (1:29, 36). The point being made by John the Baptist is that this 'Lamb' was to be killed at the Feast of Passover, a point that would not be lost on John's Jewish readers.

The meal, then, was probably a Passover Meal, but held a night earlier than the official Jerusalem Feast for one of the reasons given above. Why does John fail to identify this meal as the Passover and why does he fail to narrate the events of the Last Supper (as in the other three Gospels)? One answer may account for both questions. It is that John wants to fill the horizons of his hearers with Christ the Lamb of God, who will be sacrificed the next day, so all other details are blanched from his Gospel. The foot-washing anticipated the crucifixion of the 'Lamb of God' and Judas' betrayal brought it to pass.

Mark and John

'The disciple Jesus loved', the author of the Fourth Gospel (John 21:24), was almost certainly John Zebedee (as a process of elimination suggests: John 21:1–3). This man was present at the Thursday evening meal (John 13:23), so we must take seriously his written account of that meal. Likewise we take seriously the witness of Mark about the Passover meal. This author appears to have been present in Jerusalem at the time of Jesus' arrest (Mark 14:51–52) and, according to sober early tradition, wrote his Gospel from his associations with Peter. In other words, both John and Mark were well placed to write their respective accounts of the Last Supper.

Contradictions: between historians

Contradictions between historians are common, as in these two examples.

The first is a difference between Josephus and Tacitus over statistics. Josephus records the number of people who besieged Jerusalem in AD 66–70 as 6,000 (*War* 6.284), whereas Tacitus records the number as 600,000 (*Hist.* 5.13). There is no easy way to reconcile these divergent numbers. Is one or the other, or are both, inaccurate? Or perhaps, we do not understand the way these authors wrote numbers (which they did by using letters as symbols for numbers since numerals were not yet in use)? Either way, it would be hasty to reject the *fact* of the Roman siege of Jerusalem during AD 66–70, which is also corroborated by archaeology.

Another example is the diverging accounts of Polybius and Livy about Hannibal's crossing the Alps to invade Rome. Polybius records 12,000 African and 8,000 Iberian foot soldiers and not more than 6,000 horses (*Histories* 56.4). Livy, however, acknowledging other estimates (even citing Polybius' figures), ultimately suggests Hannibal brought 80,000 foot soldiers and 10,000 horses into Italy (*AUC* 21.38). Once again, common sense indicates that these writers probably lacked the technical means to be precise about the numbers of troops and other details. Critical analysis would study the tendencies to exaggerate in these authors and then reach an appropriate conclusion. Either way, we do not doubt Hannibal's crossing of the Alps. In any case, without Polybius and Livy there is no other way of knowing about this event.

Gospels and historical integrity

The example of the historical Jesus is interesting because we have no fewer than four Gospels.[8] Mark's, which Matthew and Luke have expanded by additions from their own special sources, and for differing audiences, is the shortest. John is written independently of the other Gospels. It is doubtful these writers would have expected us to 'harmonize' their Gospels or to set their Gospel side by side with the others.[9] Each understood that his Gospel was a sufficient portrayal of Jesus in its own right and for their specific audiences.

Each Gospel is a 'faith' document written by a 'man of faith' for gathered congregations of 'people of faith'. The Gospels are not merely information about Jesus, such as Tacitus' biography of Agricola or Suetonius' *The Twelve Caesars*. True, both of those authors had opinions about their subjects that they sought to 'bring out' in their biographies. Nonetheless these texts are *information* intensive. In the Gospels, however, the writers sought to 'bring out' the unique character of Jesus so as to inspire *faith* in him. Thus the Gospels are *faith*-intensive. True, they provide considerable historical and geographical detail as they do so, but their goal is not just to provide such detail, though the details they provide prove to be authentic.

Gospels as historically reliable biographies

Do the Gospels recount what happened during Jesus' ministry in AD 29–33, or do they reflect only the issues facing the churches at the time the Gospels were written three or four decades later?

8. There were originally six versions of the words of the prophet in the Qur'an, five of which were destroyed.
9. See C. L. Blomberg, 'The Legitimacy and Limits of Harmonization', in D. A. Carson and J. D. Woodbridge (eds.), *Hermeneutics, Authority and Canon* (Leicester: Inter-Varsity Press, 1986), pp. 145–147.

It has been fashionable for some biblical scholars to adopt the latter view, that the Gospels are not about what Jesus said *back then* but about what the gospel writers have put in his mouth about the issues the churches faced *later*.

This view, however, breaks down under the weight of contrary evidence. The letters of Paul and others in the thirty-year 'space' between Jesus and the Gospels reveal the pastoral challenges facing the churches, for example:

- The inclusion of the Gentiles: Galatians
- The eating of food offered to idols: 1 Corinthians
- Women prophesying: 1 Corinthians
- Faith without works: James
- The separation of believers from Judaism: Hebrews
- Perseverance in the face of persecution: 1 Peter

Do the Gospels portray Jesus' addressing these matters from the thirties, forties and fifties? In fact, they do not. With true if naive integrity they tell about issues Jesus addressed in the early thirties, in particular his engagement with 'sinners' and the Pharisees.

Moreover, and of great importance, the apostles clearly distinguish their words from those of the Lord (1 Cor. 7:10). The Gospels are not anachronistic, but genuine historically based biographies.

Gospel truth and atheists

Several things need to be kept in mind as we read the Gospels. First, we read them as ancient texts written at a time when resources for research and cross-checking were generally unavailable. Secondly, we read them as texts that were crafted out of the perspectives of four different personalities for distinctive audiences. Thirdly, we read them primarily as 'faith' documents, written by men of faith for people of faith. Fourthly, we recognize that, despite their diversity, they agree as to the overall sequence of events concerning Jesus.

Finally, we recognize that the primary authors Mark and John were well positioned to know the facts about Jesus, which they reproduce in the course of their respective writings.

Unless we who read the Gospels approach them in this way – New Atheists included – their message will prove to be elusive. Worse, the New Atheists will create their own criteria of historical perfection and then pronounce them erroneous. But by their methods they would have to pass the same judgment on all other texts from that era, which would mean that much of the ancient world would be a blank sheet.

We are grateful, indeed, to have the texts of Tacitus, Livy and Josephus, since without them we would have little knowledge of centuries of history in the Mediterranean world. How much more, therefore, should we be grateful for the four Gospels, which narrate the coming of the Redeemer? Those texts are written to elicit and strengthen faith, but that does not mean they are historically deficient: in fact the opposite is true.

8. THE BIRTH STORIES

And this will be a sign for you: you will find a baby wrapped in swaddling cloths and lying in a manger.

Luke

The New Atheists claim that the Gospels are 'ancient fiction',[1] and are 'most certainly not literal truth',[2] and 'cannot be introduced into a serious investigation'.[3] Harris holds the virgin birth up as 'one of the principle pieces of "evidence" demonstrating the divinity of Jesus' and then attempts to discredit it by outlining the fabrications and inconsistencies in the virgin birth stories and prophecies.[4] Together they make the (alleged) contradictions in the infancy narratives a priority.[5]

These critics point to three areas of difficulty in the nativity stories in the Gospels:

1. R. Dawkins, *The God Delusion* (London: Bantam, 2006), p. 97.
2. C. Hitchens, *God Is Not Great: How Religion Poisons Everything* (New York: Twelve, 2007), p. 120.
3. Ibid., p. 122.
4. S. Harris, *The End of Faith* (New York: Norton, 2004), pp. 94–96.
5. Ibid., p. 95; Hitchens, *God Is Not Great*, p. 111; Dawkins, *God Delusion*, pp. 93–95.

- The virginal conception of Jesus
- Contradictions between Matthew and Luke
- Incredible embellishments

The virginal conception

The Gospels present the virginal conception of Jesus as a supernatural intervention. It therefore belongs with the miracles of Jesus and his resurrection from the dead as distinctive elements that mark him out as the unique revealer of the unseen God, his only mediator with humanity.

I am not engaging with the philosophical or scientific issues associated with miracles, but will confine myself to the questions of history (see chapter 9).[6] Apart, then, from the philosophical question of the miraculous, the atheists' other main objection to the virginal conception is historical, that it is found in only two of the four Gospels and is not mentioned elsewhere in the New Testament.

It is true that only Matthew and Luke provide direct accounts of Jesus' birth. Yet the main thing they teach is that Mary was a virgin (*parthenos*: Matt. 1:23; Luke 1:27) whose conception of the child Jesus occurred without the matching engagement of a male. Matthew narrates this one way ('that which is conceived in her is from the Holy Spirit'; Matt. 1:20) and Luke another way ('the Most High will overshadow you; therefore the child to be born will be called holy – the Son of God'; Luke 1:35).

Similarly divergent are their ways of referring to the virginal conception in their respective genealogies. Matthew records as a pattern the names of 'A who was the father of B', but abruptly breaks that pattern and states that Joseph was 'the *husband* of Mary, of whom Jesus was born, who is called Christ' (Matt. 1:16). Mary was the mother of Jesus, but Joseph her *husband* was not the biological father

---

6. See further J. Lennox, *God's Undertaker: Has Science Buried God?* (Oxford: Lion, 2009), pp. 192–206.

(though he was the legal father, having named the child). In Luke's genealogy Jesus was 'the son (*as was supposed*) of Joseph' (Luke 3:23). It was *supposed* that Jesus was the son of Joseph, but that was only the outward appearance; the reality was otherwise – Joseph was not his biological father.

From the divergent genealogies and many other details it is clear that these writers did not copy from one another. Nonetheless each has his own way of establishing the supernatural conception of Jesus. Thus, to say the least, Hitchens is misleading when he claims that even 'Matthew and Luke cannot concur on the Virgin Birth.'[7] Their lack of agreement in exact words is actually evidence of their non-dependence on one another, that is, of their independence. So far from being a point of weakness it is the opposite, a point of strength, historically speaking. Exact verbal agreement might mean collusion, whereas independence points to integrity.

Each narrative is low-key and 'matter of fact' in style, unlike the mythical accounts of, for example, the birth of Augustus Caesar, whose mother was impregnated by a snake as she slept in the temple of Apollo.[8]

What, then, of the non-reference to the virginal conception in the other two Gospels? Whilst John is silent on a virgin birth, his Gospel does not explain exactly how Jesus' humanity (which is presented clearly in this Gospel) can be reconciled with his heavenly origin or pre-existence (which is equally clearly presented). John does not introduce Jesus until he was an adult, yet he is simultaneously presented as 'of Nazareth' (John 1:45–46), 'the son of Joseph' (John 6:42) *and* as having been 'with God' in the beginning (John 1:1) and 'from above' and not of this world (John 8:23). John does not explain the paradox that Jesus is both from heaven and truly a man, but the virginal conception satisfies that paradox.

7. Hitchens, *God Is Not Great*, p. 111.

8. Suetonius, *Aug.* 2.94. Suetonius derived this from *Theologymena* by Asclepias of Mendes (now lost).

John writes in an allusive, often symbolic way. His description of a believer's spiritual ('virginal') rebirth 'not of blood nor of the will of the flesh nor of the will of man, but of God' (1:13) seems to be based on the virginal conception of Christ.

John's unusual language describing one's supernatural entry into the family of God at the same time aptly describes the virginal conception of the Son of God.

There is no way of knowing why Mark is silent about the virginal conception or, for that matter, any other aspect of the nativity of Christ. Joseph's name does not appear in the Gospel of Mark, but that does not necessarily imply the virginal conception, but rather that Joseph was probably dead when Jesus began his ministry. All we can say is that Mark portrays Jesus as a man of action who bursts on the scene as an adult and disappears as dramatically as he appeared. Absence of detail about his prior life is matched by the emptiness of the tomb after his death.

How valid is the claim that the rest of the New Testament makes no reference to the virginal conception? In answer I point out that these other New Testament writers effectively teach a heightened message about Christ, his pre-existence, birth and redemptive death that is consistent with the manner of his supernatural birth. Paul taught the 'incarnation' of the Son of God from his pre-existent deity to his human life, culminating in his degradation in crucifixion (Phil. 2:5–8; 2 Cor. 8:9) and that 'when the fullness of time had come, God sent forth his Son, born of woman, born under the law, to redeem . . . ' (Gal. 4:4–6; Paul's words could be a summary of Luke 2 – 3). Peter and the writer to the Hebrews give the same 'cosmic' message about the pre-existent Christ that is consistent with the Gospels' narrative of the virginal conception (1 Pet. 1:18–21; Heb. 1:1–4).

So while it is true that there are only two direct narratives of the first Christmas, the writings of Paul, Peter, the letter to the Hebrews, John and Paul are consistent with the main emphasis of those narratives: the virginal conception of the Son of God.

Contradictions between Matthew and Luke

Nazareth or Bethlehem?

The biggest problem in the accounts is that Matthew already has Joseph and Mary in Bethlehem when Jesus was born, whereas Luke narrates their journey *from* Nazareth to Bethlehem. According to Luke's account, Joseph, Mary and Jesus returned to Nazareth from Bethlehem after a brief visit to Jerusalem. In Matthew, however, the family fled from Bethlehem to Egypt and, it appears, would have returned to Bethlehem but settled in Nazareth in Galilee only because Archelaus was ruling Judea in his father Herod's place. These awkward details call for discussion.

It seems that Matthew and Luke each wrote his Gospel not depending on the other but on oral or written sources that had arisen between the nativity of Christ and the time when Matthew and Luke began to write their Gospels many years later. Since Mark does not begin his narrative until Jesus' baptism as an adult, it is certain that Mark was not amongst the sources for Matthew's and Luke's birth stories. It is possible, even likely, that the differences between Matthew and Luke were already embedded in the sources available to them.

This probably meant that neither Matthew nor Luke knew the source(s) available to the other. At the same time, each writer naturally sought to emphasize this aspect or that in the conversion of their sources into their respective final narratives, according to their perceptions of the needs of their readers. Matthew wrote for Jewish readers, and Luke for Gentiles, which explains why these texts 'feel' so different to us.

Their varying audiences would have involved Matthew and Luke's omitting material or amplifying it. It is worth noting that Matthew and Luke wrote their respective Gospels *seventy* or so years *after* the birth of Jesus. It seems that neither Matthew nor Luke knew the detailed contents of the other since neither attempted to harmonize or correct the other's narrative.

Thus Matthew's omission of the journey from Nazareth to Bethlehem could be explained by a source that did not know of the journey; or that Matthew chose not to report it for the sake of brevity; or because he wanted to emphasize Micah's prophecy that the Messiah would be born in Bethlehem (Matt. 2:6; Mic. 5:2). Silences are not necessarily contradictions.

Gender emphasis in Matthew and Luke

It is well known that Matthew's nativity stories focus on *Joseph*, with minimal reference to Mary (see e.g. Matt. 1:18–25; 2:13, 19–23). How can we explain this? Was it the case that Joseph passed on these stories to his *sons*, including to his second son, James, who was destined to become the leader of the Jerusalem-based, Jewish Christianity? Did James become a source for Matthew in the writing of his Gospel, at least regarding the birth stories? Was Matthew's interest in Joseph rather than Mary because his Gospel was *Jewish* and *male*-orientated?

By contrast, Luke's Gospel is well known for its interest in the roles of women (see e.g. Luke 2:36–38; 7:37–50; 8:2–3; 10:38–42; 23:27, 49; 24:1–3; 24:9–11). Consistent with this, Luke narrates his Gospel from Mary's viewpoint (see Luke 1:39–56; 3:51). Luke's observation that Mary 'treasured these things in her heart' (Luke 2:51) implied that somehow he, the narrator, came to know about 'these things'. We know that Luke was in Judea for three years in the late 50s, providing him the opportunity to know about Jesus' birth details, either directly from Mary or indirectly from those (women?) she had confided in.

There are also stylistic differences between Matthew and Luke. Luke wrote in terms of Old Testament birth narratives. Mary's Song (Luke 1:46–55) echoes Hannah's song at the birth of Samuel (1 Sam. 2:1–10). Matthew's style is less poetic but concerned to demonstrate that Jesus fulfilled the prophecies from the Old Testament (Matt. 1:22; 2:6, 18, 23).

Genealogies

These and other reasons help explain why Matthew and Luke are so distinct in some details. Amongst the differences none is so striking as their genealogies. Matthew begins with Abraham and moves forward to Jesus, whilst Luke begins with Jesus and moves backward to Adam. Moreover the names in their lists do not coincide, making it impossible to reconcile them.

Thus the genealogies represent another possible contradiction between Matthew and Luke that New Atheists seize as evidence of inaccuracy. Many have attempted to solve these different lists of names, but without success. The genealogies are almost completely divergent and have not been reconciled despite many efforts to do so.

Either way, it must be understood that genealogies generally at that time were by no means precise. They tended to be selective, with names included or excluded to make a point. The sources Luke and Matthew used were probably differing village archives, which they adapted according to their respective outlooks and objectives.

Matthew's genealogy is organized in three sets of *fourteen* generations (Abraham to David; David to the exile; the exile to Christ). Matthew would have known that there were many more generations within these periods. His use of 'fourteen' was deliberately symbolic. At a time before numerals were used, letters served as numerals. We note that the number 'fourteen' could be represented by the letters DVD, clearly referring to David who was the ancestor of the Christ. This device is called gematria and was used by the rabbis, which reminds us that genealogies were often selective and imprecise.

Matthew's genealogy begins with Abraham (reflecting his *Jewish* readership), whereas Luke's goes back to Adam (representing a non-Jew's *universal* audience).

Core agreements

Despite these considerable differences in detail and style and divergent genealogies, there is remarkable underlying historical agreement between Matthew and Luke (see table 8.1 below).

Table 8.1 The birth of Jesus: core details

	Matthew	*Luke*
Jesus was born in Bethlehem	2:1	2:2
In the time of Herod (d. 4 BC)	2:1	1:5
His mother was Mary (betrothed to Joseph)	1:18	1:26; 2:5
His legal father was Joseph (who named the child)	1:18	1:26
But not the biological father	1:16, 20, 22	1:34; 3:23
Jesus was raised in Nazareth in Galilee	2:22–23	2:39
From the line of David	1:1	1:32

In other words, these independent Gospels written to ethnically different audiences agree about the core facts concerning the birth of Jesus.

Embellishments

What about 'Christmas card' items in the nativity narratives?

Magi

'Magi' (wise men) were Mesopotamian students of astrology and astronomy who would have been expected to be interested in spectacular 'signs' in the heavens, especially when such signs were held to be portents of great events. According to Matthew, they 'saw his star when it rose' (Matt. 2:2), suggesting they followed the direction of the heavenly lights. As many have observed, the biblical record does not say there were three Magi.

One of the great prophecies of the Old Testament, which would affect not only the Jews, but also the whole world, concerned a star. According to Numbers 24:17, 'a star shall come out of Jacob, / and a sceptre shall rise out of Israel'. Centuries before Christ, the Jews interpreted this to mean that a ruler for the whole world would arise from the Jewish people. The Greek translation of the Old Testament, for example, translates Numbers 24:17 as, 'a star shall come forth out of Jacob, / a *man* shall arise ... '

A hundred years after Christ, Rabbi Akiba saw the rebel leader ben Kosiba as that 'star' who would rule Israel. Akiba renamed him bar Kokhba, 'son of a star'.

The Gentiles also knew of this Jewish prophecy. Tacitus writes of 'a mysterious prophecy ... of the ancient scriptures of their priests' whereby 'the Orient would triumph and from Judea would go forth *men* destined to rule the world'.[9] Tacitus changed the prophecy from the singular 'man' to the plural 'men', seeing the fulfilment in father and son Vespasian and Titus, who, as the Roman victors of the Jews in AD 66–70, were both destined to become emperors. It is probable that the Magi from Mesopotamia knew a version of this prophecy.

Every 805 years the planets Jupiter and Saturn draw near to each other. Astronomers have calculated that in 7 BC the two planets were 'massed together' three times: in May, September and December, and that in February, 6 BC, they were joined by Mars, presenting a spectacular triangular conjunction.[10]

It is possible that the Magi, knowing the ancient 'star' prophecy, on seeing the brilliant planetary formation and a comet decided to visit Judea to see the new king of the world. In 1871 the astronomer John Williams published his authoritative list of sightings of comets. Comet number 52 on Williams's list appeared for seventy days early in 5 BC and would have been visible in the Middle East.[11] Was this the 'star' that guided the Magi?

Time magazine, in its cover story of 27 December 1976, commented that while 'there are those who dismiss the star as nothing more than a metaphor ... others take the Christmas star more literally, and not without reason. Astronomical records show

---

9. Tacitus, *The Histories*, tr. K. Wellesley (Harmondsworth: Penguin Classics, 1964), 5.13.
10. See P. L. Maier, *The First Christmas* (London: Mowbrays, 1971), pp. 69–88.
11. See J. Finegan, *Handbook of Biblical Chronology* (Princeton: Princeton University Press, 1964), pp. 245–246.

that there were several significant celestial events around the time
of Jesus' birth.'

Shepherds: Luke 2:8–20

As with other parts of the Christmas story, the gospel writer Luke
weaves a 'message' into the incident about the shepherds. In that
society shepherds were typically uneducated and spent their days
caring for sheep and goats. It was deeply symbolic that these lowly
herdsmen should witness the Lord's epiphany and be told of the
birth 'this day' of a Saviour, Christ the Lord, the 'sign' of which was
that the newborn child would be lying in a manger (a stone trough
for feeding farm animals). Luke skilfully brings out the match
between the lowliness of the shepherds and the humble circumstances of the birth of the Christ child.

There is no reason to doubt the essential storyline of this incident.
To this day shepherds tend flocks of sheep and goats in Israel and
Jordan, including around Bethlehem. Unlike other countries, where
farm dogs and motorbike riders control sheep, in the Middle East
(where there are usually no fences), sheep are always watched over
and cared for by shepherds.

Evil King Herod: Matthew 2:7–12

How credible is the account of Herod's ordering the killing of the
baby boys of Bethlehem? Herod was king of the Jews from 37 to
4 BC, and throughout his long reign had arranged the murder of a
wife, Mariamne (he had nine wives altogether), and two of his sons.
Augustus Caesar joked that it was 'safer to be Herod's pig than
Herod's son'.[12] The king was scrupulous not to break the Old
Testament ban on eating pork but cared little about the sixth
commandment.

Knowing his own death was near, Herod ordered the arrest of
the distinguished men from every village of Judea (Josephus, *War*

---

12. Macrobius, *The Saturnalia*, tr. P. V. Davis (New York: Columbia
University Press, 1969), p. 171 (2.4.11).

1.660). He ordered that at his death these men were to be executed. At least tears would be shed – if not for his passing, then for the massacre of these popular leaders. When the king died the order was not carried out, but the incident shows that the one who was capable of issuing it was also capable of 'the slaughter of the innocents'.

Matthew's report about the arrogance and cruelty of the king of the Jews is to establish a dark backdrop against which to set the brightness of the humility and worship of the gentile Magi. Matthew is anticipating the future worship of Christ the king by the peoples of the nations.

At the same time, however, we see a thread of historical truth binding this story together.

Conclusion

Typical of their approach elsewhere, the New Atheists seize the loose threads in biblical history and attempt to tear apart the whole garment. That there are details to seize cannot be denied, yet upon closer inspection the threads prove to be secure within the integrity of the cloth.

So, while it is true that only Matthew and Luke, two of the four Gospels, narrate the virginal conception, it does not follow that it did not happen. John does not directly 'narrate' the virginal conception, but it is implicit in his Gospel. How else could he explain the phenomenon of Jesus who existed in eternity with God but who became truly a man? Furthermore references by Paul, Peter and Hebrews to the pre-existence of the Son of God are consistent with the virginal conception as the explanation of the coming of this cosmic figure into our world.

Moreover the supposed 'differences' between the nativity stories in Matthew and Luke, so far from damning their accuracy are actually evidences of their underlying historical truth. Those differences are striking, including their irreconcilable genealogies, the silence of

Matthew about the journey from and back to Nazareth, Matthew's Israel-centred and Luke's world-centred perspectives, Matthew's focus on Joseph against Luke's focus on Mary, and their quite different narrative vocabularies.

These differences may have been embedded in the sources Matthew and Luke received when they came to write their Gospels seventy or so years after the birth of Jesus. Alternatively these writers expressed their differences out of their own perceptions about Jesus and their understanding of the needs of their readers, who for Matthew were Jews and for Luke, Gentiles.

Nonetheless, despite these extensive differences in their texts as we have them, these writers reflect a remarkable agreement about the core historical elements. Mary, the betrothed of Joseph of the line of David, who fell pregnant not by man but by the Holy Spirit, gave birth to her child in Bethlehem during the reign of Herod the king, whereupon the parents raised this child in Nazareth in Galilee.

Elements in the story, so easily regarded as fictional embellishments, on further examination prove to be historically consistent. There were such people as Magi, astronomers from Mesopotamia, and there were rare astral phenomena in about 6 BC. Shepherds were commonplace and Herod was as evil in reality as Matthew portrays him to have been.

Nonetheless these Gospels do not set out to be 'straight' biographies of Jesus. Matthew wants us to see Joseph as a humble and godly man and the Magi as dutifully worshipful of the Christ child in contrast to the wily and cruel Herod, who sought to destroy Christ. Luke portrays the woman Mary as mystified by her unexpected pregnancy, yet obedient to God. Humble shepherds join these homeless parents at the animal's food trough where the child was laid, all due to the decree of an uncaring and distant world ruler. The nativity stories are profoundly challenging, both morally and spiritually, revealing the 'humility' of God in his purposes for the world. Yet running through these narratives is the cord of historical truth.

9. MIRACLES

*Hume's scepticism about cause and effect and his agnosticism about the
external world are of course jettisoned the moment he leaves his study.*

Anthony Flew

Such was the influence of the philosopher David Hume (1711–
76) that Dawkins could claim that 'The nineteenth century is
the last time when it was possible for an educated person to
admit to believing in miracles like the virgin birth without embarrassment.'[1] That embarrassment would extend to the miracles
at the hands of Jesus. Many notable scientists such as Graeme
Clark and Francis Collins would be quick to reject Dawkins's
assertion.

Hume's argument was based on human experience and observation. Based on experience, Hume argued, people conclude that
things always happen in a predictable way; for example, the sun
will rise tomorrow. 'Uniform experience' reaches a level where
there is no room for doubt. By contrast, the evidence for miracles
can never be strong enough to convince modern people, especially

---

1. R. Dawkins, *The God Delusion* (London: Bantam, 2006), p. 187.

since they are said to have occurred amongst 'ignorant and barbarous nations'.[2]

Ancient does not mean 'ignorant and barbarous'

It is far from true that the era of the Gospels was 'ignorant and barbarous'. The Greeks, whose writings, when rediscovered, were the inspiration for the Renaissance and the beginnings of modernity, faced deep philosophical and moral issues. With engineering precision the Romans skilfully erected great buildings such as the domed Pantheon in Rome, which still stands majestically despite the passage of two millennia. The writers of the Gospels employed carefully crafted grammatical sentences in narratives whose depth and subtlety have only recently come to be appreciated.

Furthermore people in that era were aware that a miracle was just that: a miracle. The Jewish Sadducees rejected outright the idea of the resurrection (Acts 23:8) and the philosophers of Athens, based on the long-held certainty that the dead stay dead, laughed at Paul's assertion of a coming resurrection of the dead (Acts 17:32). According to Greek thinking, there is no resurrection of the dead (as reflected in Paul's references to Corinthian scepticism: 1 Cor. 15:12). Luke, a physician, records the disbelief of Zechariah that his hitherto barren wife, Elizabeth, could bear a son (Luke 1:20). It is simply not true that all people in the era of the New Testament were gullible.

Modern people should avoid classifying people of Greco-Roman antiquity as ignorant and unscientific. If, for example, these peoples had the use of Arabic numerals, instead of having to use letter equivalents for numbers, their advances in technical matters may have accelerated progress and anticipated modernity. Whilst advances in knowledge continued through late antiquity into the

---

2. Quoted Lennox, *God's Undertaker: Has Science Buried God?* (Oxford: Lion, 2009), p. 194.

Middle Ages, it is arguable that the era of Jesus was more advanced in many fields than comparable fields in the tenth century, a millennium later would be. Progress is not inevitable or uniform; regress sometimes happens.

In this regard, Christians in the Middle Ages may have been more gullible about miracles than people in the apostolic era. John Moschos, a monk, records his travels in the Judean desert in AD 600 in his book.[3] As well as providing a window into Christian monasticism in that era this account also strikes us as superstitious because of the remarkable frequency of visions and miracles. Although the Venerable Bede writes in a more objective way, based on his wide reading, his *History of the English Church and People* (written in the early eighth century) is likewise punctuated by a plethora of miracles we modern people find difficult to accept. By contrast, the era of the New Testament many hundreds of years earlier does not appear to have been so prone to find the miraculous in the ordinary course of life.

Scientist Francis Collins believes in God but adopts a rigorous attitude to the frequency of miracles:

> It is crucial that a healthy scepticism be applied when interpreting potentially miraculous events, lest the integrity and rationality of the religious perspective be brought into question. The only thing that will kill the possibility of miracles more quickly than a committed materialism is the claiming of miracle status for everyday events for which natural explanations are at hand.[4]

This sober attitude is consistent with the cautious reporting of the miracles of Jesus in the Gospels. The miracles of Jesus in the Gospels are striking, but not bizarre, unlike an apocryphal gospel of later

---

3. J. Moschos, *The Spiritual Meadow* (Kalamazoo, Mich.: Cistercian, 1992). William Dalrymple, *From the Holy Mountain* (London: Flamingo, 1996), reports how he retraced the steps of John Moschos.

4. F. Collins, *The Language of God* (New York: Free Press, 2006), pp. 51–52.

centuries which recorded that the boy Jesus made twelve sparrows out of clay and then commanded them to fly away (*Inf. Gosp. Thom.* 1).[5]

Miracles, regularity and singularity

Against Dawkins, who follows Hume, Lennox points out that for the Gospels to mention a miracle 'there must have been some perceived regularity to which that event is an apparent exception! You cannot recognise something as abnormal if you do not know what is normal.'[6]

C. John Collins writes in a similar vein:

> Hume's reasoning overlooks one very important fact, namely, the normal reason for telling a story is to report 'interesting' or 'tellable' events, not the *usual* ones. This means that a narrative will not be about what we know already. This leads to another flaw in Hume's case: a consistent application of Hume's ideas would leave us doubting all historical accounts of unusual things.[7]

Lennox makes the important distinction between the 'uniformity of nature', based on observation, and *absolute* uniformity, based on

5. The Qur'an also appears to include this story: God will say, 'Jesus son of Mary, remember the favour I bestowed on you and your mother: how I strengthened you with the Holy Spirit, so that you preached to men in your cradle and in the prime of manhood; how I instructed you in the book of Wisdom, in the Torah and in the Gospel; *how by My leave you fashioned from clay the likeness of a bird and breathed into it so that, by My leave, it became a living bird;* how by My leave, you healed the blind man and the leper, and by My leave restored the dead to life . . . ' (*The Koran*, tr. N. J. Dawood [London: Penguin, 2000], 5:110, italics added).

6. J. Lennox, *God's Undertaker: Has Science Buried God?* (Oxford: Lion, 2009), p. 199.

7. C. J. Collins, *The God of Miracles: An Exegetical Examination of God's Action in the World* (Wheaton: Crossway, 2000), p. 167, italics original.

a singular event that had not been observed. He is referring to the 'Big Bang', by which the universe is thought to have begun, a singular unrepeatable and unobserved event.

> For in modern science there are central ideas that appear contrary to our experience. A strict application of Hume's principles might well have rejected such ideas, and thus have impeded the progress of science! It is often the counterintuitive anomaly, the contrary fact, the exception to the past repeated observation and experience, which turns out to be the key to the discovery of a new scientific paradigm.[8]

The Creator and miracles

Hume and his followers regard nature as 'uniform' and closed, so that miracles would 'violate' the laws of nature. The requirement that nature be uniform, however, is really an argument for an external mind or force that has created and maintained that uniformity. The Mind that regulated the uniformity in nature, as we observe it, must have the power to intervene in nature, by a miraculous action.

Rather than treating a miracle as a violation of nature, it is better to regard it as a divine 'interference' (following C. S. Lewis), to which the usual processes of nature then adapt. A divine interference initiated Mary's pregnancy, but the usual 'natural' processes of the created order then took their course and the child was born nine months later. God initiated acts of healing at the hands of Jesus that accelerated the healing processes that routinely happen.

Colin Brown concurs:

> Left to her own devices, we would expect nature to behave normally. Nature could not do anything but that. But if God is God, and if God is the author of nature, then occasionally when it suits his purpose, we

---

8. Lennox, *God's Undertaker*, pp. 205–206.

might have to reckon with God's doing things that we had never seen before.[9]

Lennox writes similarly:

if, in order to account for the uniformity of nature, one admits the existence of a Creator, then that inevitably opens the door for the possibility of a miracle in which the Creator intervenes in the course of nature. There is no such thing as a tame Creator who cannot or must not, or dare not intervene in the universe he has created . . .

I conclude, therefore, that there is no scientific, in-principle objection to the possibility of miracles. Surely, then, the open-minded attitude demanded by reason is now to proceed to investigate the evidence, to establish the facts, and be prepared to follow where that process leads, even if it entails alterations to our *a priori* views.[10]

That evidence is *historical* evidence and it is extensive and compelling. Observations from science are able to lead an atheist to theism or deism, but not necessarily to personal faith in the Creator. Once again, now in relationship to miracles, the question of gospel truth becomes paramount.

Historical evidence for miracles

Later Jewish sources

The non-Christian sources Josephus and the Talmud refer to Jesus' miracles. Josephus, writing in the 90s, states that 'Jesus . . . wrought surprising feats.'[11] The Talmud, written much later, says that 'they

---

9. C. Brown, *That You May Believe* (Grand Rapids: Eerdmans, 1985), p. 32.

10. Lennox, *God's Undertaker*, pp. 205–206.

11. Josephus, *Antiquities of the Jews*, tr. L. H. Feldman, LCL (Cambridge, Mass.; Heinemann, 1965), 18.63 (Gk. *paradoxōn ergōn*).

hanged Yeshua because he practised sorcery',[12] a probable reference
to the accusation that he performed exorcisms by the power of the
devil (Mark 3:22).

Such references are unlikely to have arisen from Christian sources
but from within Jewish traditions that were hostile to Jesus and that
originated amongst his opponents and critics. Their hostile nature
adds weight to their credibility, especially when read alongside the
accounts of miracles in the Gospels. The Gospels record Jesus'
miracles positively and the Jewish traditions record them negatively;
these are multiple but opposite interpretations of events that speak
of an underlying historical reality.

The sayings of Jesus in the Gospels
The *sayings* of Jesus about miracles imply their historicity. John
the Baptist from prison sought assurances that Jesus was in fact the
Christ. Jesus replied, 'Go and tell John what you have seen and heard:
the *blind* receive their sight, the *lame* walk, *lepers* are cleansed, and the
deaf hear, the *dead* are raised up, the *poor* have good news preached
to them' (Luke 7:22 / Matt. 11:4–5).

Joachim Jeremias, an authority on Aramaic language, argued that
these words, which Jesus originally spoke in Aramaic, occurred in a
poetic speech rhythm characteristic of the way Jesus spoke.[13]

Similarly formulaic are Jesus' reported words about his activities
in three major towns in the region at and near the lake:

> Then he began to denounce the cities where most of his *mighty works* had
> been done, because they did not repent. 'Woe to you, Chorazin! Woe to

---

12. *B. Sanh.* 43a. *The Talmud of Babylonia: An American Translation*, tr.
    J. Neusner, T. Zahavy, et al. (Atlanta: Scholars Press for Brown Judaic
    Studies, 1984–95). For further (late) Jewish references to Jesus'
    miracles see B. Blackburn, 'The Miracles of Jesus', in C. A. Evans and
    B. Chilton (eds.), *Studying the Historical Jesus* (Leiden: Brill, 1994),
    pp. 353–394 (361).

13. J. Jeremias, *New Testament Theology*, vol. 1 (ET London: SCM, 1971),
    p. 21.

you, Bethsaida! For if the *mighty works* done in you had been done in Tyre
and Sidon, they would have repented long ago in sackcloth and ashes . . .
And you, Capernaum, will you be exalted to heaven? You will be brought
down to Hades. For if the *mighty works* done in you had been done in
Sodom, it would have remained until this day.' (Matt. 11:20–23)

These well-rounded words call for explanation. How did they come
to be recorded unless Jesus did 'mighty works' in those three towns?
How did they assume a rounded poetic form unless they had come
to be recited from earliest times?

This reference is historically credible. In Galilee the Jewish popu-
lations were concentrated around the north-west quadrant of the
lake (where Chorazin, Bethsaida and Capernaum were located). The
south-west quadrant was dominated by Tiberias, the tetrarch's capital
built in AD 17 near burial grounds and therefore ritually offensive to
Jews. The south-east quadrant belonged to the Decapolis and was
a predominantly Gentile region. The north-east quadrant, although
ruled by Philip, a Herodian prince, was significantly Hellenized with
a somewhat lesser Jewish representation than in the north-west.
Archaeology reveals a concentration of synagogues in the north-
western quadrant, a smaller component in the north-eastern
quadrant but significantly fewer in the other two.[14] Jesus' words
about three towns in the Jewish dominated north-western quadrant
of the lake are geographically consistent.

The saying is also geographically credible. Chorazin was only a
few kilometres to the north of Capernaum, and Bethsaida a few
kilometres to the east, across the Jordan within Trachonitis–Iturea.
Although we do not know the exact location of Bethsaida, its name
(House of Fishermen) demands that it was close to the lake.

Furthermore Jesus' words are consistent with his declared
priority for 'the lost sheep of the house of Israel' (Matt. 10:6;

---

14. E. M. Meyers and J. F. Strange, *Archeology, the Rabbis and Early
    Christianity* (London: SCM, 1981), fig. 7; J. J. Rousseau and R. Arav,
    Jesus and His World (Minneapolis: Fortress, 1995), p. 271.

cf. Mark 7:57). Accordingly, as in Mark's narrative, Jesus began to preach in synagogues in Capernaum and the immediate vicinity, such as Chorazin and Bethsaida, but was forced further afield by the opposition of the local religious leaders and the menace of the tetrarch. Ultimately this meant travel beyond Antipas' jurisdiction into the regions of Tyre, Sidon, Trachonitis–Iturea and the Decapolis. In other words, this saying represents a genuine oracle from the earlier period of Jesus' ministry to three adjacent settlements: Chorazin, Bethsaida and, in particular, Capernaum.

The number and diversity of miracles in the Gospels

The sheer number and diversity of Jesus' miracles, as recorded in the Gospels of Mark and John and the sources underlying the Synoptic Gospels,[15] is overwhelming (see table 9.1 below).[16]

Table 9.1 Miracles in the Gospels

Gospel	Number of miracles	References
Mark	20	
John	7	
Q	1	(Luke 7:1b–10 / Matt. 8:5–13)
M	2	(Matt. 9:32–34)
L	3	(Luke 5:1–11; 7:11–17; 17:11–21)

It appears that altogether there are independent references to more than thirty miracles at the hands of Jesus. Mark and John did not depend on one another nor did the sources that underlie Matthew and Luke (Q, L, M).

---

15. The source common to Matthew and Luke is known as Q, and the sources peculiar to Matthew and Luke are known respectively as M and L.

16. For a schedule of the miracles see E. Ashley, 'The Miracles of Jesus', in M. Harding and A. Nobbs (eds.), *The Content and Setting of the Gospel Tradition* (Grand Rapids: Eerdmans, 2010), pp. 395–416.

Furthermore it is no less striking that we find a *diversity* of four different kinds of miracles across Mark and John and the Synoptic sources (Q, L, M), in total no fewer than five independent sources (see table 9.2 below).

Table 9.2 Multiple attestation of four miracle types

	Mark	*John*	*Q*	*L*	*M*
Exorcisms	Capernaum demoniac (1:21–28) Gerasene demoniac (5:1–20)				The dumb demoniac (9:32–34; cf. 10:5–8)
Nature miracles	Stilling the storm (4:35–41) Feeding the 5,000 (6:30–44) Walking on the water (6:45–52) Withered hand (3:1–6)	Feeding the 5,000 (6:1–13) Walking on the water (6:16–21) Official's son (4:46–54)	Centurion's boy (Matt. 8:5–13)	Draft of fishes (5:1–11) Bent woman (13:10–17)	
Healings	Blind Bartimaeus (10:46–52)	Man born blind (9:1–34)			
Resurrections	Daughter of Jairus (5:21–43)	Lazarus (11:1–44)		Widow's son (7:11–17)	

The range of miracle types (exorcisms, nature miracles, healings, resurrections) is thus attested independently across these sources. According to Barry Blackburn, 'the miracle-working activity of Jesus – at least exorcisms and healings – easily passes the criterion of multiple attestation'.[17] J. P. Meier devoted five hundred pages to reviewing Jesus' miracles and declared their multiple attestation to be 'massive'.[18] One witness to the miracles of Jesus would be questioned, but at least two for each kind of miracle is a challenge to a mind that is open to the consideration of historical evidence.

Miracles in the time of Jesus

Sceptics tend to dismiss the miracles of Jesus by arguing that 'miracles' were commonplace in that era. It is agreed that both the Jews and the Greco-Romans were often superstitious and preoccupied with irregular phenomena to assist them in making important decisions. Contemporary Jewish attitudes are evident in Josephus' fascination with portents at many points, for example, in overnight storms,[19] weird phenomena in the heavens or mysterious happenings in the temple.[20] Though an intelligent man and an observant Jew, Josephus was deeply influenced by portents and signs.[21]

However, this does not necessarily mean that 'miracles' were everyday phenomena as is often assumed. Following are some of the more prominent miracle-workers from the era of Jesus:

---

17. B. Blackburn, 'The Miracles of Jesus', in C. A. Evans and B. Chilton (eds.), *Studying the Historical Jesus* (Leiden: Brill, 1994), p. 356.
18. J. P. Meier, *A Marginal Jew: Rethinking the Historical Jesus*, vol. 2 (New York: Doubleday, 1994), p. 631.
19. Gk. *terata*.
20. See *War* 4.287; 6.288–300; 6.292.
21. Josephus, the Jewish historian and propagandist, wrote from Rome in the last thirty years of the first century.

1. The holy rabbi Honi, the Circle-Drawer, also known as Onias (first century BC),[22] was said to have successfully prayed for rain, not merely for a downpour or a drizzle but 'a rain of grace'.[23]

2. John the disciple drew Jesus' attention to a man who was casting out demons in Jesus' name.[24] It was not the *fact* of the exorcisms but that they were done in Jesus' name that caused John's comment. Josephus reports witnessing a Jewish exorcist named Eleazar drawing a demon through a man's nostrils and consigning it to a basin of water.[25] Evidently, exorcisms were not unheard of or exceptional.

3. Rabbi Gamaliel, the teacher of Saul of Tarsus, once prayed during a storm at sea, whereupon the sea subsided.[26]

4. In the AD 70s the devout rabbi Hanina ben Dosa prayed for the dangerously ill son of his teacher, Yohanan ben Zakkai, and the boy lived.[27]

These phenomena, which were relatively uncommon, were unlike the miracles of Jesus. Jesus' miracles were immediate and direct, based on his authoritative words. The 'miracles' of rabbis like Hanina ben Dosa were mostly answered prayers.

When the evidence for 'miracles' in Jesus' time is investigated, they prove to be relatively infrequent, apart from exorcisms. Nonetheless, despite the relative rarity of reported miracles in Jesus' era in Israel, the suspicion remains for some that the gospel writers invented miracles and attributed them to Jesus as a miracle-worker, to validate the claims about him. However, the number (thirty plus) of Jesus' miracles and their wide diversity recorded across a fivefold range of sources is powerful evidence of their historicity.

---

22. Josephus, *Ant.* 14.22.
23. *M. Ta'an.* 3.8.
24. Mark 9:38.
25. Josephus, *Ant.* 8.46–49.
26. *B. Meṣi'a* 59b.
27. *B. Ber.* 34b.

Miracles and the character of Jesus

Jesus did not perform miracles to make money, or to gain power over people, or to secure a favourable political outcome. Yet there is evidence from that era of those who attempted to work wonders for just those motives. Simon the magician sought to make himself more powerful over people by even greater magic, which he would pay money to acquire (Acts 8:9–11). Paul's opponents in Corinth passed themselves off as touched by divine power to gain influence over the Christians in that city (2 Cor. 2:17; 5:12; 11:5, 14, 20). Religious charlatans such as the Egyptian prophet attempted to re-enact the 'signs' of Moses and Joshua to force out Roman occupying forces (Acts 21:38; Josephus, *War* 2.261–263; *Ant.* 20.169–171). The attempted use of 'unusual' powers for self-serving purposes is still with us, as are their gullible victims.

Jesus' miracles were invariably done out of compassion for the diseased, the hungry and the fearful. Furthermore his miracles did not violate the 'good' in creation, where healing routinely occurs within the body and where storms eventually cease. Under Jesus the good purposes of God were focused and accelerated for the benefit of others. Jesus' miracles pointed to the goodness of the Creator, to his unique sonship of that Father, and were signs that his kingdom had indeed come, and of hope that it would come in all its fullness, when injustice, pain, crying and death will be no more.

The Gospels and their sources

It is quite acceptable to say that Mark's Gospel was written before AD 70 and the other three within a decade or so. This means that the time between Jesus and these texts was thirty to forty years. The Gospels, however, were not merely writing about Jesus on the further side of a three- or four-decade-wide chasm, detached from him (see fig. 9.1 below). Rather, each author wrote his Gospel out

of source material that had been assembled for mission purposes
in the years since Jesus. Whilst some of this mission source material
was in oral form, other material was written, as Luke indicates (Luke
1:1–4).

29–33	33–65	65–80
Jesus' words and works	Oral and written sources	The Gospels

Fig. 9.1 Timeline from Jesus to the Gospels.

The Gospels are each 'mission literature', the final 'written up'
version of 'mission resources' that arose out of and subsequent to
Jesus' mission in Israel.

Case study: the feeding of the five thousand

The feeding of the five thousand is one of a select number of
miracles reported in the independent Gospels Mark and John. Due
to the sources on which these Gospels depend, and due also to their
individual ways of narrating this incident we note slightly different
storylines and different vocabulary, but identical statistics (5,000
men, 5 loaves, 2 fishes and 12 baskets). Clearly it is the same incident
(see table 9.3 opposite).

John and Mark broadly have the same sequence, but in John's
Gospel it is Jesus who welcomes the crowds, whereas in Mark's the
people arrive before him. According to John, Jesus does nothing
with the crowd before the feeding, but in Mark he teaches them.
In Mark's account the disciples confront Jesus with the problem of
the hungry crowd, but in John it is Jesus who asks Philip how to
feed them. Mark does not name any disciples, but John names Philip
and Andrew. In John there is a 'boy' as a key detail; there is no 'boy'
in Mark.

These and other variations in detail, along with quite distinctive
vocabulary (such as John's *'barley* loaves' and *'pickled* fish') are
evidence that John has not adapted Mark's version of the miracle
nor vice versa.

Table 9.3 Independent accounts of the feeding of the five thousand

Mark 6:30–44	John 6:1–14
Journey by boat to a lonely place followed on land by a crowd from the cities running to get there first. Out of compassion Jesus teaches the crowd.	Journey across lake to other side; Jesus sits on mountain, sees crowd following; Passover.
Because it was late and a lonely place, the disciples tell Jesus to send them off to buy food.	From the mountain Jesus asks Philip how to feed them.
Jesus to the disciples, 'You feed them,' and they say 200 *denarii* are needed.	Philip: 200 *denarii* are needed.
Jesus asks, 'How much food?' They reply, '5 loaves and 2 fishes.'	Andrew: 'A boy with 5 barley loaves and 2 pickled fish.'
The multitude are seated on *green* grass in companies.	5,000 seated on *much* grass.
Jesus looks to heaven blesses, breaks, gives to *disciples* to distribute.	Jesus takes the bread, gives thanks and *he* distributes.
All eat and are satisfied, with 12 baskets (*kophinoi*) surplus collected by disciples.	All eat and are satisfied. Jesus instructs disciples to gather up remains, 12 baskets (*kophinoi*).
Jesus forces disciples into boat, says farewell to the crowd, goes to the mountain to pray.	Crowd acclaim him as the prophet and attempt to force kingship on him; Jesus goes to mountain to pray.

Logically we conclude that there were two parallel tradition streams of this miracle, oral or written, that Mark and John have independently written up as part of their respective Gospels. Mark and John have shaped and expressed their Gospels according to their perception of the pastoral needs of their respective audiences. John appears to have written for Jewish Christian congregations, whilst Mark seems to have written for Gentile Christian congregations.

Miracles in Mark, Matthew and Luke

This idiosyncratic 'shaping' of their received traditions is pertinent to these authors' way of writing about the miracles of Jesus. Matthew and Luke follow Mark's portrayal of Jesus as the herald of the imminent coming of the kingdom of God. The evidence of the in-breaking kingdom of God, said Jesus, was his victory over unclean spirits: 'But no one can enter a strong man's house and plunder his goods, unless he first binds the strong man. Then indeed he may plunder his house' (Mark 3:27).

Other words of Jesus indicate that he regarded the messianic age as having come (prophesied in Isa. 35:4–6), as witnessed by his miracles (also as noted above) (see table 9.4 below).

Table 9.4 Messiah's miracles

Luke 7:22 / Matthew 11:4–5	*Isaiah 35:4–6*
'Go and tell John what you have seen and heard:	'"Behold, your God will come with vengeance,"
the *blind* receive their sight,	with the recompense of God.
the *lame* walk,	He will come and save you.
lepers are cleansed	Then the eyes of the *blind* shall be opened,
and the *deaf* hear,	
the *dead* are raised up,	and the ears of the *deaf* unstopped;
the *poor* have good news preached to them.'	then shall the *lame* man leap like a deer, and the tongue of the *mute* sing for joy.'

More tersely Jesus comments that the kingdom of God is present with them:

> Being asked by the Pharisees when the kingdom of God would come, he answered them, 'The kingdom of God is not coming with signs to be observed, nor will they say, "Look, here it is!" or "There!" for behold, the kingdom of God is *in the midst* of you.' (Luke 17:20–21)

To summarize, Mark, followed by Matthew and Luke, report Jesus' miracles as tangible evidence that the kingdom of God has materialized in Jesus. He is the bearer and executor of the end-time rule of God.

Miracles in the Gospel of John

John, however, focuses even more on Jesus' miracles than the other Gospels do (John 20:30–31). He presents these as 'signs' that he is the Son on earth of the heavenly Father who sent him, and that his 'works' are the works of the Father. To see Jesus at work in a miracle is to see him doing the 'works' of his Father. In short, John's emphasis is on Jesus as the Christ, the Son of God who perfectly reveals the unseen God.

Miracles in the Gospels: the assumption of truth

The point to be made here is that the Gospels do not argue for the *fact* of the miracles of Jesus, but merely assume that they had happened. Mark (followed by Matthew and Luke) shapes his source material about Jesus' miracles to establish that Jesus is both herald and bearer of the coming kingdom of God. John, however, shapes his source material to establish that Jesus is the Son of his heavenly Father on earth.

It is more than likely that these writers have merely confirmed the emphases embedded in the sources they received. They are unlikely arbitrarily to have imposed novel interpretations on the miracles. Indeed, it is almost certain that Mark and John were themselves deeply involved in the formation of the traditions they finally converted into their gospel texts.

The ease with which these writers narrate the miracles without apologetic argument suggests that the truth of the miracles had come to be accepted in the communities to which those early sources had been directed. The final versions of the tradition in the written Gospels by no means exert apologetic pressure within the texts to convince the readers about the historicity of the miracles of Jesus.

Conclusion

To deny the existence of the Creator, atheists old and new must argue that the universe created itself and that its intricacy and order were the result of blind chance. It is pointed out that atheists, therefore, are people of faith since they *believe* this is how and why things are. That belief, however, rests on an unproven supposition and theory.

Contrary to assertions of atheists that modern science has dispensed with God and that religion is finished, it is nonetheless a fact that as many notable scientists today believe in the Creator as their counterparts did a century ago, proportionally speaking.[28] Furthermore there is no evidence of the disappearance of religion; quite the contrary in fact, for example in 'secular' China, where Christianity is growing rapidly.[29]

The observations of scientists like Clark, Collins and Lennox point to the reality of the Creator, his amazing intelligence and power. They would be the first to acknowledge, however, that scientific arguments for God do not of themselves connect us with God in a personal way. It is only the gospel of God, his message focused on Jesus, that does that in and for us.

The miracles focused *on* Jesus – his virginal conception and his resurrection – were God's way of marking him out as unique, as a prophet, but infinitely more than a prophet: as the incarnate Son of God. So too the miracles *by* Jesus point to him as the heaven-sent Son of God, Son of Man and Messiah.

In turn, this raises the question of evidence – historical evidence – for the miracles of his birth and resurrection and the miracles that occurred at his hands. In chapter 8 I presented some of the reasons for believing the miracle of his birth, and in chapter 10 I will point to some of the evidence for his resurrection. In this chapter I

---

28. See Lennox, *God's Undertaker*, pp. 17–19.
29. This is the argument, statistically supported, of J. Micklethwait and
    A. Wooldridge, *God Is Back* (London: Penguin, 2009).

identified the fivefold independent witnesses to at least thirty miracles, and to their remarkable diversity, witnessed by a range of independent sources. Not least important is the moral character of Jesus' miracles as 'signs' of his compassion, his unique relationship with the Creator and as windows into hope for humanity.

10. THE RESURRECTION OF JESUS OF NAZARETH

When the dust hath drained the blood of a man, once he is slain, there is no resurrection.

Aeschylus

It is understandable that the New Atheists' attack on God is directed at the miracles in the New Testament. To destroy their credibility would effectively destroy any notion that Jesus was the Son of God, the unique revealer of the unseen Creator. The whole structure of historic Christianity depends on the historical truth of the miracles.

This viewpoint, however, is an inference, for the New Testament writers do not say this directly. They merely *narrate* the virginal conception of Jesus, his miracles and his resurrection from the dead. It is only after further reflection on these events that we understand that the miracles *in* Jesus (his conception and resurrection) and the miracles *by* Jesus (*his* miracles) mark him out as the unique man, unique in the true meaning of that word.

In chapters 8 and 9 I addressed the virginal conception and miracles of Jesus respectively. Now I address the question of the resurrection of Jesus of Nazareth, following his crucifixion. There is a striking symmetry here. Whereas his conception was supernatural, his birth was natural. By reverse, his death was natural, his resurrection supernatural.

As with the miracles of Jesus' conception and with his supernatural 'signs', the prior question is, 'Are miracles possible?' That answer depends on whether or not one believes in the Creator. If one holds that the creation has generated itself and that its intricacy is the result of blind chance, then one would be bound to reject miracles. If, on the other hand, one were open to a theistic explanation of the phenomena of life in the universe, openness to the possibility of miracles would follow. Nonetheless a theistic belief would not mean an uncritical acceptance of every miraculous claim.

Miracles are not merely 'coincidences' or unexpected and unusual happenings we can explain by psychological processes. Rather miracles are *events* so contrary to the usual created order, upheld by God, that they can be explained only as a suspension of that order by special divine action. In this understanding, the miracles by Jesus in the Gospels are indeed miracles, but none more so than his resurrection.

The natural and observable order of life is that animals, including people, die and do not rise bodily to continue living. The word 'bodily' is important here since 'the resurrection of the dead' literally means, 'the standing up of corpses'. Thus understood, 'resurrection' cannot mean something merely emotional or 'spiritual', for example in the memories of those who mourn a deceased person. To say 'Elvis lives' is not the same as saying that 'Jesus was raised from the dead'!

Jesus' resurrection from the dead is so astonishing a miracle that it demands exceptional evidence.

Evidence in Paul: the Jerusalem tradition

It is widely accepted that Paul's letters are datable and that their dating makes them the earliest surviving documents of Christianity. In AD 50 Paul came to Corinth in southern Greece, where he established a church. In his letter written a few years later he reminded the members of the core message he 'handed over' to them, which they 'received' (1 Cor. 15:3–7).

Paul summarized that message as follows:

> Christ *died* for our sins in accordance with the Scriptures, that he was *buried*, that he was *raised* on the third day in accordance with the Scriptures, and that he *appeared* to . . . more than five hundred brothers at one time, most of whom are still alive . . .

Paul did not formulate these words, but 'received' them already formatted within five years or less of Jesus' death (in AD 33). Paul does not indicate who created this brief summary, but the most likely suggestion is that it arose within the Christian community in Jerusalem. Did Paul 'receive' this creed-type statement at the time of his baptism in Damascus (in AD 34) or when he returned first to Jerusalem (in AD 36)? Either way, this oral formula embedded in an early letter takes us back to the time immediately after Jesus.

Here Christ's *death*, *burial*, *resurrection* and *appearances* to people are stated as historical facts. The *burial* confirmed the fact of the *death*; the *appearances* confirmed the fact that he *was raised*. Further evidence for his resurrection was provided by 'he was raised on the third day'. 'On the third day' specifies the point of time, three days (according to Jewish internal counting) after his death and burial. That he 'was raised' (i.e. by God) 'on the third day' is a specific statement that is to be taken literally.

It is sometimes pointed out that Paul does not specifically refer to the empty tomb in this passage. Nonetheless his summary of the 'received' gospel that Christ *died*, was *buried*, was *raised* and *appeared* to particular people implies that the burial tomb was empty. For Christ to be 'raised' and to 'appear' to people means that he was no longer in the tomb; hence it is evident that the tomb was empty.

We assume that when he returned to Jerusalem, Paul checked carefully about the empty tomb and the authenticity of the resurrection appearances. Humanly speaking he had everything to lose and nothing to gain by converting to Christianity. It is unlikely that so intelligent and logical a person as he was would have turned his whole life upside down if he had any lingering doubts about the resurrection of Jesus.

Paul nowhere attempted to prove that Jesus rose again from the dead. Paul knew this had happened; there was no need to argue the point. In one of his earliest letters written in AD 50, only seventeen years after the crucifixion, Paul reminded the Thessalonians that 'Since we believe that Jesus died and rose again, even so, through Jesus, God will bring with him those who have fallen asleep' (1 Thess. 4:14). Paul and his readers believed Jesus died and rose again. Based on that agreed fact Paul adds something the Thessalonians did not yet properly grasp, that God would bring back the deceased believers with Jesus at his return. It is clear from the following words that the Thessalonians had come to believe in the death and resurrection of Jesus through Paul's visit:

> The word of the Lord sounded forth from you . . . how you turned to God from idols, to serve the living and true God, and to wait for his Son from heaven, whom he *raised from the dead*, Jesus who delivers us from the wrath to come. (1 Thess. 1:8–10)

This is clear evidence that in AD 50 it was Paul's practice to proclaim publicly that Jesus had died but was then 'raised' from the dead.

Between Jesus and the Gospels: living traditions

The resurrection references in Paul's letters establish that the apostle and his churches believed that Jesus had been resurrected from the dead. New Atheists and liberal scholars say that the Gospels and their resurrection stories were written many decades after Jesus and that the space between Jesus and the Gospels was a blank space, that their accounts of sightings of the resurrected Jesus were just stories made up when the Gospels were written.

But this goes against the evidence from the letters of Paul, Peter, James and the letter to the Hebrews that were written as mission literature within the space between Jesus and the writing of the Gospels (see fig. 10.1 below). Those letters indicate that the resurrection of Jesus was a central plank in their beliefs.

29–33	33–65	65–80
Jesus	The apostles' letters	The Gospels

Fig. 10.1 Timeline: Jesus, the letters of the New Testament and the Gospels.

The letters of the early leaders Paul, Peter, James and the writer to the Hebrews point to vigorous church life within the three or so decades separating Jesus from the writing of the Gospels. During that period the oral and written traditions about Jesus were formulated and used in various expressions of Christian ministry so that they were living traditions when the gospel writers wrote them into the texts as we have them. This applies specifically to the gospel accounts of the appearances of the resurrected Jesus.

Evidence in the Gospels

Although the Gospels were written 30–40 years after Jesus' lifespan, they depended on sources that had been developed in the intervening years. As mentioned in chapter 9, there were five such sources:

- Mark
- Q (material common to Matthew and Luke)
- L (material found only in Luke)
- M (material found only in Matthew)
- John

The text of Q, as reconstructed from Luke and Matthew, ends before Jesus arrived in Jerusalem. It does not cover the events of Jesus' death, his burial, the empty tomb or the resurrection appearances. Thus we eliminate the Q source, which means we have four sources relevant to the death of Jesus, his burial, the emptiness of the tomb and his appearances.

Mark and John are the final, written-up form of their own separately channelled traditions. Matthew and Luke enclose within them two separately channelled traditions, L and M. These four separate sources of information for the death, burial, resurrection and appearances of Jesus had been formulated in the three or four decades between Jesus and the final written versions of the Gospels (see fig. 10.2 below).

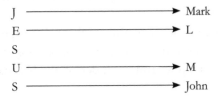

Fig. 10.2 The formulation of the Gospel traditions.

The point to make is that these channelled sources are independent of each other, like separate silos of information. The different vocabulary in each demonstrates that none of these sources has copied from the other. Thus there are, in effect, four independent witnesses to the final events of Jesus, his death, burial, the empty tomb and his resurrection appearances (see table 10.1 below).

Table 10.1 Independent sources for Jesus' death, burial, empty tomb and resurrection appearances

	Mark	*L*	*M*	*John*
Death	15:37	Luke 23:46	[Matt. 27:24–25]	19:30
Burial	15:46	Luke 23:53	[Matt. 27:64]	19:42
Empty tomb	16:6	Luke 24:2, 10, 12, 23		20:2, 6
Appearances	14:28; 16:7	Luke 24:12, 15, 36	Matt. 28:9–10; 16–17	20:14, 19, 26; 21:14

The Gospels do not overtly set out to match the death, burial, tomb emptiness and resurrection appearances, as in the Jerusalem tradition Paul quotes in 1 Corinthians 15:3–7 (see above). Nevertheless the four Gospel sources when analysed indicate a similar underlying fourfold pattern (death, burial, empty tomb, resurrection appearances), a pattern that appears also in the final written-up narratives of the Gospels. The single exception is that the Matthew source (M) does not refer to the empty tomb. This is not a fatal objection, however, since M's references to Jesus' resurrection appearances following his burial presupposes the emptiness of the tomb.

The agreement between the tradition Paul quotes and the tradition common to the four sources underlying the Gospels is astonishing, and a powerful reminder of the historicity of these events.

It is no less remarkable that witnesses are *named* for each of the four events. This is important because a named person implies the possibility of checking the details, especially if that person is eminent. These witnesses may have been alive when the Gospels were written.

In the analysis below (see table 10.2 opposite), the striking thing is that so notable a person as Joseph of Arimathea, a member of the Sanhedrin in Jerusalem, provided a tomb for the burial of Jesus. This is a detail that could be verified or falsified.

It is of special significance that the name of Mary from Magdala (near Tiberias) appears as a witness in *each* source for *each* of the sequences of events. We assume that the witness of Mary of Magdala to these key events made her a significant figure in earliest Christianity.[1] The names of people found in the Gospels are probably an indication of their high profile in the early church. Furthermore each of the other female witnesses is carefully identified by a qualifying remark, for example Mary *the mother of Joses*. The names cited in

---

1. See R. Bauckham, *Jesus and the Eyewitnesses* (Grand Rapids: Eerdmans, 2006), pp. 39–66.

Table 10.2 Names of witnesses of Jesus' death, burial, empty tomb and resurrection appearances

	Mark	*L*	*M*	*John*
Death				Mary (mother of Jesus), Mary (wife of Clopas), Mary Magdalene, the beloved disciple
Burial	Joseph of Arimathea, Mary Magdalene, Mary (mother of Joses)			Joseph of Arimathea, Nicodemus
Empty tomb	Mary Magdalene, Mary (mother of James), Salome	Mary Magdalene, Joanna, Mary (mother of James), Peter		Mary Magdalene, the beloved disciple, Peter
Appearances	[Peter]	Clopas and companion		Mary Magdalene, Thomas (with ten named disciples, Peter, the beloved disciple)

the Gospels mean the writers were submitting their texts to the test of accountability.

As many have observed, it is remarkable that the Gospels' witness to the death, burial, tomb emptiness and resurrection of Jesus depends to the degree that it does upon the testimony of women such as Mary of Magdala, Joanna and the various other women. The testimony of women was not generally admissible in court, as

Josephus observed: 'From women let no evidence be accepted
because of the levity and temerity of their sex' (*Ant.* 4.219).[2]

The prominence of the witness of women to these events is
striking and quite unexpected. If such evidence had been contrived
it would not have been attributed to the testimony of women in the
Jewish culture of that period.

The Jerusalem tradition and the Gospel sources

It is not possible to harmonize the sequence of appearances of the
risen Jesus as we have them in the Gospels and in the early Jerusalem
tradition, quoted by Paul in 1 Corinthians 15:3–7:

he was raised			
	he	appeared	to Cephas
then			to the twelve
Then	he	appeared	to more than 500 . . .
Then	he	appeared	to James,
then		to all the apostles	

In common with the Gospels, Paul's tradition indicates a sequence
of the 'appearances' of the resurrected Christ and also supplies
names of the witnesses – Cephas (Peter), James and the twelve, names
that were accessible to enquiry.

The difficulty of harmonizing the underlying sources has been
pointed to as evidence of unreliability. It should be mentioned,
however, that the gospel writers were not setting out to prove or
even systematically to narrate the history of Jesus' resurrection
appearances. These authors write from the assumption that their
readers know about and believe the resurrection.

---

2. Tr. L. H. Feldman, LCL (Cambridge, Mass.: Heinemann, 1965).
   Women were amongst those who were ineligible to report the
   beginning of a new moon (*m. Roš Haš.* 1.8).

Furthermore the existence of 'loose ends' is evidence that these writers had not contrived a harmonious, even account. The discrepancies are a reason to believe in the naive integrity of the writers and, indeed, are not unusual in writers of the period. The historians who narrate the great fire of Rome in AD 64 disagree about Nero's whereabouts during the fire and whether he 'fiddled' (played the lyre) or sang while the city burned. Yet no one doubts that Nero failed to show leadership while a raging fire was destroying the city.

A senior judge commented similarly regarding evidence in trials:

> Courts expect honest and reliable witnesses to agree in substance but differ in detail and view with suspicion witnesses who give exactly the same evidence. The Gospels are four substantially independent accounts which agree in substance, but differ in details, and they pass this test.[3]

A realistic approach to history would accept variations of detail in the accounts of the resurrection appearances of Jesus. But for the New Atheists these variations are proof of the fundamental unreliability of the New Testament. Dawkins chides 'unsophisticated' Christians who think the Bible a literal and accurate record and hence 'evidence supporting their religious beliefs' by asking, 'why don't they ever notice those glaring contradictions?'[4] Hitchens throws his hands up in the face of these differences: 'If the apostles do not know or cannot agree, of what use is my analysis?'[5] These supposed contradictions provide incontrovertible evidence to Hitchens that religion is man-made.[6]

In fact, however, the variations in detail are just what we would expect in traditions that had developed independently and that were

3. K. Handley, 'The Evidence for the Resurrection – a Judge's View', *Global Journal of Classic Theology* 7.3 (2009), p. 6.

4. R. Dawkins, *The God Delusion* (London: Bantam, 2006), p. 94.

5. C. Hitchens, *God Is Not Great: How Religion Poisons Everything* (New York: Twelve, 2007), p. 115.

6. Ibid.

finally written down for differing audiences. So far from these
variations being signs of weakness they are actually evidences of
historical strength.

In short, the resurrection appearances of Jesus to so many
people and at different times and places as recorded in the oral
tradition and the Gospel sources argues powerfully for the truth of
the resurrection.

Circumstantial matters

No expectation of an individual's resurrection
Jews of the era of Jesus believed in the resurrection, but it was a
resurrection of everyone who had died beforehand (Ezek. 37:1–14).
The bones of the deceased were placed in small containers called
ossuaries, awaiting the universal resurrection. The words 'resurrection of the dead' meant 'the standing up of *corpses*' (plural) ahead
of the last judgment of all people. Jews did not find any reference
in the prophetic scriptures to the resurrection of an individual.
Martha, sister of the deceased Lazarus, declared that 'he will rise
again in the resurrection on the last day' (John 11:24).

The suggestion that the disciples made up the story of the resurrection of Jesus to fit in with current expectations is not sustainable.
There was no such expectation. In fact, the resurrection of Jesus
took the disciples completely by surprise. Even when the risen Lord
stood in front of them we read that 'some doubted' (Matt. 28:17).

'Kings', 'prophets' and the survival of earliest Christianity
It may come as a surprise to know that Jesus was not the only famous
leader amongst the Jews of first-century Palestine. The historical
writings of the Jewish writer Josephus are dominated by his references to self-styled 'kings' and 'prophets' who arose in the first
century.

After the death of Herod the Great in 4 BC a period of instability
followed. Three men arose, each claiming the title 'king': Judas in

Galilee, Simon in Perea, Athronges in Judea.[7] After a period of bloody warfare Simon was killed, Athronges was captured and their respective followers were dispersed, allowing the Herodian princes at last to take over their respective sections of Herod's kingdom. The 'kings' Simon and Athronges are long forgotten apart from Josephus' brief descriptions.

Judas the Galilean, who survived the wars of 4 BC, was a rabbi who led an uprising in AD 6 against the Roman annexation of Judea as a Roman province.[8] Judas and the Pharisee Saddok established a new zealot-like activist movement called 'fourth philosophy' that advocated violent action rather than submission to Gentile rule, which the payment of taxes to Rome was seen as implying. The Romans quelled this uprising and killed its leaders, but it was, in effect the beginning of a conflict with the Romans that reached its climax in the war of AD 66–70.

Sixty years later, Judas's son Menahem captured Masada, and, duly armed, 'returned like a veritable king to Jerusalem'.[9] Since Judas proclaimed himself 'king' in 4 BC and his son Menahem returned like a 'king' to Jerusalem in AD 66, we are able to identify an aspiring dynasty of kings in this Galilean family. This dynasty, likewise, is long forgotten.

In the fifties and sixties, when relationships between the Jews and Romans in Judea had deteriorated even further, there were increasing manifestations of revolutionary factions such as the Sicarii and the Zealots. These also crumbled before the military might of Rome or destroyed one another in bloody cross-factional struggles.

During the period AD 40–70 a succession of prophetic figures such as Theudas, who attempted to part the waters of the Jordan, arose and the 'Egyptian' prophet who sought to make the walls of

---

7. For Judas see Josephus, *War* 2.56; *Ant.* 17.271–272. For Simon see *War* 2.57; *Ant.* 17.271–272; Tacitus, *Hist.* 5.9. For Athronges see *War* 2.60–65; *Ant.* 17.278–284.

8. Josephus, *War* 2.118; 7.253; *Ant.* 18.4–10, 23–25; Acts 5:37.

9. Josephus, *War.* 2.433 (Thackeray, LCL).

Jerusalem collapse.[10] The Romans quickly destroyed these and similar 'sign' prophets, and they are also long forgotten.

The revolutionary groups and the prophetic movements did not survive the AD 66–70 war with the Romans. Apart from Josephus' accounts, the only traces in history of their heroism for the cause of God are the coins they minted during the war, the ashes from the Sicarii stronghold at Masada, the remains of the Jerusalem temple and the arch erected in Rome by Titus, their conqueror, celebrating their defeat! No literature expressing their hopes or beliefs has survived.

What, then, of the other three 'philosophies' – as Josephus calls them – current in the time of Jesus? Apart from the 'first philosophy', the Pharisees, the other 'philosophies', the Sadducees and the Essenes,[11] did not survive the AD 66–70 war. After the war the Pharisees evolved into non-violent rabbinic Judaism and produced the literature of the Mishnah and Talmud. Apart from the Pharisees Christianity was the only known movement within Judaism to survive the AD 66–70 Jewish war with Rome.

Why did Christianity survive within that first, critical century, when all other movements except rabbinic Judaism did not?

The answer lies in the massive personal impact of Jesus on his disciples and his resurrection from the dead. No doubt that personal impact remained with his first disciples. It was not this, however, that they proclaimed, but his resurrection from the dead.

It was his resurrection that caused his personal qualities to be remembered and his sayings to be treasured and written down. It was because he rose from the dead that his missionary movement began and the Gospels were written. If Jesus had not been raised from the dead, he and his teachings would have faded from their

---

10. For Theudas see Josephus, *Ant.* 20.97–99; 20.167–168; *War* 2.258–259; for the Egyptian prophet see *War* 2.261–263; *Ant.* 20.169–171; Acts 21:38.

11. Josephus, *War* 2.119–161; *Ant.* 18.18–22; Pliny, *Nat.* 5.15.73; Philo, *Hypoth.* 11.1–18; *Prob.* 12–13.

minds, would not have been remembered and would not have been committed to writing. Jesus would have been just another mistaken prophet or activist, forgotten beyond his immediate generation.

The otherwise unaccountably changed lives of James, Peter and Paul

Three of those named as having seen the risen Christ – James, Peter and Paul – died as martyrs within just over three decades after the resurrection. James was executed in Jerusalem in AD 62 at the hands of the high priest Annas II, Peter and Paul, in Rome in the mid-sixties under Nero Caesar.[12]

We are able to follow the life and movements of James and Peter over the previous thirty-five years and those of Paul over the previous thirty years. The records are extensive.

It is remarkable that these men, who were to become mission leaders as a result of the change the risen Christ had made in their lives, did not apparently know one another beforehand. Nor were

---

12. Josephus, *Ant.* 20.200, records the death of James between the period in office of the governors Festus and Albinus. Written *c.* AD 95, 1 Clem. 5 implies that Peter and Paul were executed under Nero: 'But not to dwell upon ancient examples, let us come to the most recent spiritual heroes. Let us take the noble examples furnished in our own generation. Through envy and jealousy, the greatest and most righteous pillars [of the church] have been persecuted and put to death. Let us set before our eyes the illustrious apostles. Peter, through unrighteous envy, endured not one or two, but numerous labours, and when he had finally suffered martyrdom, departed to the place of glory due to him. Owing to envy, Paul also obtained the reward of patient endurance, after being seven times thrown into captivity, compelled to flee, and stoned. After preaching both in the east and west, he gained the illustrious reputation due to his faith, having taught righteousness to the whole world, and come to the extreme limit of the west, and suffered martyrdom under the prefects. Thus was he removed from the world, and went into the holy place, having proved himself a striking example of patience' (M. W. Holmes, *The Apostolic Fathers* [Grand Rapids: Baker, 1999]).

they agreed about all things as leaders of the various mission groups. Differences of opinion, even quarrels between them, are a matter of record.[13] But they were united in their belief in and proclamation of the resurrection of Jesus.[14]

Critical questions are posed by the lives of these men. Why did James, Jesus' younger brother, who did not originally believe in Jesus (John 7:5), *become* his devoted servant after the first Easter? Why did Peter, after Jesus' death, *continue* to serve him, apparently having expected the apocalyptic kingdom of God to intervene when Jesus arrived in Jerusalem?[15] Why did Paul, having been a zealous persecutor of Jesus' followers, *begin and continue* to serve him at such great personal cost?[16]

The resurrection of Jesus from the dead is critical to these questions. Peter would not have continued, nor would James and Paul have begun, to serve Jesus unless these men were convinced Jesus had been raised from the dead.

James remained in Nazareth with his brothers, sisters and Mary after Jesus moved to Capernaum to commence his public ministry in Galilee. There is evidence of resentment, or even of hostility, towards Jesus (Mark 3:21, 31–35). Yet, after the first Easter, James became a member of the church in Jerusalem, then the first of its three 'pillars', then its sole leader.[17] This otherwise unknown man from Nazareth became leader of a community of many thousands in Jerusalem, a man who became respected in the wider community.[18]

Peter's changed life direction from that of an obscure fisherman in the landlocked Sea of Tiberias to that of sect leader in Jerusalem calls for explanation, as do his world travels from Galilee through

---

13. See Gal. 2:11–14; 1 Cor. 1:12; 9:5; Acts 21:18–21.
14. 1 Cor. 15:5, 7–8, 11.
15. Luke 22:38, 49; 24:21; John 18:10; Acts 1:6.
16. Gal. 1:13–16.
17. Acts 1:14; 12:17; Gal. 1:19; 2:9; Acts 15:13; 21:18.
18. Josephus, *Ant.* 20.200.

Judea, Samaria, Syria, Asia Minor, Greece to Italy and also his author-itative encyclical to the Anatolian provinces.

Consider, too, the radical turnaround of *Saul* the obsessive protector of the faith of his fathers who, as a leading scholar and activist, sought to destroy the heretical sect associated with Jesus. This man became the leading promoter of the faith he had attempted to destroy and did so among the Gentiles, a people who, as a strict Pharisee, he would have despised for their idolatry and promiscuity. How can we account for this astonishing change? In his own words, it was because the Lord, who had been raised on the third day, appeared to him (1 Cor. 9:1; 15:8–9).

James, Peter and Paul each served the risen Lord for about thirty years, James in Judea, Peter and Paul on the world stage. It is difficult to believe that they would have done this unless they were convinced that Jesus was, indeed, the risen Lord. Is it possible for *each* to have been so mistaken for *thirty* years? Remember that they were not members of a single tightly knit group, but robust individuals who operated in separate missions and were often at odds with one another.

The moral tone of their letters suggests clear thinking and burning integrity, not delusion or deceit.

The lives and the deaths of James, Peter and Paul are credible circumstantial evidence, consistent with the more direct evidence above, for the historicity of the resurrection of Jesus.

The unaccountably changed attitudes of the early Jewish disciples

The existence and growth of the sect of the Nazarenes

The earliest disciples continued to live as observant Jews, attending the synagogues on the Sabbath and the temple at the prescribed hours of prayer (Acts 3:1; 10:3). At the same time, however, they met separately in houses in Jerusalem on the first day of the week and were given the name 'Nazarenes' due to their affiliation with Jesus of *Nazareth* (Acts 24:5). Within a short time the Antioch

branch of the disciples' movement were labelled *Christianoi* (followers
of Christ) because of their loyalty to the crucified king of the
Jews, the *Christos* (the Christ). These disciples known as *Nazarenes*
and *Christians* took their names from Jesus of *Nazareth*, who was
the *Christ*.

In other words, the *Nazarenes* belonged to a subset within Judaism
along with other groups such as the Pharisees, Sadducees, Essenes
and the 'fourth philosophy' (revolutionaries). While those groups
had historic founders, it was their *ideology* that distinguished them in
the era of Jesus. With the disciples, however, the thing that distinguished them was their overt commitment to the Nazarene who had
been crucified as the Christ. Their attachment to him was primarily
personal, not ideological.

This connection with him, however, was not with a deceased
martyr but one whom they proclaimed to be the risen and exalted
Lord and to whom they prayed (e.g. Acts 2:36; 3:14–15). Given the
Jewish sense of shame associated with crucifixion, the continuance
and growth of the sect of the Nazarenes is inferential evidence of
the resurrection of Jesus from the dead.

Group inclusion 'in Christ'

Quite soon apostolic writers were referring to the Christians everywhere, as well as in local congregations, as those who were 'in Christ'.
True, the term is also used of an individual believer being a man or
woman 'in Christ'. But there are numerous examples in the writings
of the New Testament where we find a sense of corporate inclusion
under the lordship of Christ. We think, for example, of Paul's use
of *temple* and *body* metaphors, and of John's account of believers
'abiding in' Christ as 'branches' in the 'true vine' (1 Cor. 3:16; 12:27;
John 15:4).

The point is that this sense of corporate inclusion in Christ
corresponded with, but exceeded, the sense the Israelites had of
being the one covenant people of the Lord where, for example, they
were also called by such corporate terms as the Lord's *vine*, his *bride*
and his *servant* (Ps. 80:8–14; Jer. 3:14; Isa. 49:3).

Since these monotheistic Jewish Christian writers saw Christ relating to his corporate people in ways corresponding to the Lord's relationship corporately with Israel, we must conclude that these writers believed Christ to be an exalted figure, thus presupposing his resurrection.

Continuity

Radical examples of Jesus' teaching that are beyond dispute historically continued into the post-resurrection church.

One was his reference to God in the vernacular Aramaic as *abba* (father), which we see embedded in the Greek text of several of Paul's letters, where this familial approach to God was evidently common-place among Greek-speaking disciples in distant provinces. *Abba*, 'dada', corresponds with *imma*, 'mama', as an intimate way of addressing parents. The weight of scholarly opinion is that such a close and personal way of speaking to the Almighty was almost unheard of in Jewish piety. Clearly, though, Jesus' *Abba*, 'Father', became the *Abba*, 'Father,' of non-Jewish believers in Galatia and Rome.

Another example was Jesus' definitive way of declaring *Amēn* as the prefix to his weighty teachings. Jesus' use of the prefixed *Amēn* is without parallel among the rabbis and had the effect of declaring a truth of God as by a solemn oath, implying that the Lord God himself was endorsing this teaching. Without further explanation Paul merely informs the Corinthians that Christ himself is the 'yes' to all the Lord's promises in the Scriptures, and for this reason believers utter the *Amēn* to God through him (2 Cor. 1:20). Again, we observe the seamless continuity between the words of the pre-crucifixion Jesus and the practices of post-crucifixion believers.

A final example is Jesus' calculated call of *twelve* disciples, with Jesus himself as their head. Here we see his implicit messianic claim, as one who was at that time restoring the twelve tribes to Israel. Without interruption we notice that the earliest church determined to have twelve apostles in continuity to those twelve disciples (Acts 1:12–26).

Each of these examples of continuity presupposes the reality of the resurrection. Mindful of these and similar phenomena Professor

C. F. D. Moule famously asked, 'If the coming into existence of the Nazarenes . . . rips a great hole in history, a hole the size and shape of the Resurrection, what does the secular historian propose to stop it up with?'[19]

Moule raised another question about how to account historically for the novel character of the texts of the New Testament. The answer, he said, 'seems to be a most powerful and original mind [Jesus], and a tremendous confirmatory event [his resurrection]'.[20] It was the resurrection of Jesus that confirmed the 'powerful and original mind' of the pre-resurrection Jesus.

Summary

Of what value is circumstantial evidence? Kenneth Handley, a leading Australian jurist made this observation. 'The point about circumstantial evidence is the way the circumstances can sometimes fit together and point to the same conclusion.'[21] He cites the standard direction to juries in criminal cases about circumstantial evidence as given by Pollock CB in 1866 in the English case of *Regina* v. *Exall*:

> It has been said that circumstantial evidence is to be considered as a chain . . . but that is not so, for then, if any one link broke, the chain would fail. It is more like the case of a rope composed of several cords. One strand of the cord might be insufficient to sustain the weight, but three stranded together may be quite of sufficient strength. Thus it may be in circumstantial evidence – there may be a combination of circumstances, no one of which would raise a reasonable conviction, or more than a mere suspicion, but the whole, taken together, may create a strong conclusion of guilt . . . with as much certainty as human affairs can require or admit of.[22]

---

19. C. F. D. Moule, *The Phenomenon of the New Testament* (London: SCM, 1967), p. 3.
20. Ibid., p. 17.
21. Handley, 'Evidence', p. 11.
22. Ibid.

In relation to the resurrection of Jesus, Justice Handley concludes, 'The circumstantial and other evidence points to only one conclusion, that Jesus died and came back to life, and the combined strength of the evidence is very great.'[23]

Other explanations

A number of alternative explanations have been offered to the witness of the New Testament that Jesus was raised from the dead.

A hoax

The resurrection of Jesus was unexpected. Jews were expecting a resurrection, but it would happen at the *end* of history and would involve *every* person who had ever died. The scepticism of Thomas to resurrection reports was probably a typical reaction. To assert that *one* person had been raised permanently and bodily *that* day was unexpected.

Likewise to the Greeks of the period who believed in a soul's immortality the declaration that a man had been resurrected was not credible (Acts 17:32).

In short, the hoax explanation assumes ready acceptance of what is proposed, but this was not the case with Jews or Greeks.

Another man was crucified

The Qur'an teaches that Jesus was a prophet. Since God would not allow his prophet to be treated that way, another man was crucified in Jesus' place. It states, 'They did not kill [Jesus] nor did they crucify him but they thought they did.'[24]

This goes against the evidence. It was precisely because Jesus was a public figure in Jerusalem that the temple authorities and

---

23. Ibid.
24. Sura 4.156 (*The Koran*, tr. N. J. Dawood [London: Penguin Classics, 2000]).

Romans wanted him out of the way. Thousands of Jewish pilgrims congregated in Jerusalem at Passover time. Past events had shown that the tiniest spark could ignite riot and tumult in so volatile a situation.

Although Jesus was arrested at night, tried before a hastily convened Sanhedrin and then brought to Pilate in the early hours of the morning, the execution was in public. Jesus, with two revolutionary activists, was crucified close to the walls of Jerusalem, near a well-used thoroughfare (John 19:20; Mark 15:29).

The point of crucifixion was to humiliate the criminal *publicly* so as to deter others from rash behaviour. There is every indication that it was Jesus who was crucified. Those who mocked him identified him as he hung on the cross, 'He saved others . . . ' (Mark 15:31). Roman soldiers were present guarding the crucified men. It was Jesus who was crucified, not another man.

Jesus did not actually die on the cross

The 'swoon' theory was argued in the early 1800s by German scholars Venturini and Paulus and later by the British scholar Duncan Derrett.[25] Jesus became unconscious on the cross, but revived in the tomb.

This theory ignores Roman practice. The Jewish historian Josephus records many instances of Roman crucifixion in Palestine. Not only was crucifixion itself violent in the extreme; it was preceded and accompanied by brutal torture. Roman soldiers took advantage of the vulnerability of the victims. Taken together, the scourging and the nailing up of the victim represented an overwhelming assault on the human frame that left the person critically weakened. Those not already dead would have died upon removal from the cross.

If the executioners broke the legs, the victims had no leverage and thus could not breathe; death came quickly. This is precisely

---

25. J. D. M. Derrett, *The Anastasis: The Resurrection of Jesus as an Historical Event* (Shipton-on-Stour: Drinkwater, 1982).

what the Roman soldiers began to do late on that Friday afternoon. Bodies left impaled on the Sabbath during Passover brought defilement to the land. When the Jews requested that the three men be killed so as to permit burial before the onset of the Sabbath, the Roman soldiers began to break the legs of the victims.

When they came to Jesus, however, they found that he was already dead. One of the execution squad thrust a spear into Jesus, to establish that he was in fact dead, as he appeared to be. The sudden flow of blood and water was taken to be evidence of the reality of the death. Although the dead do not bleed, the blood often remains liquid in the arteries for some hours following death by asphyxia. Depending on the organs or the blood vessels pierced, water and serum could indeed issue from someone recently deceased, especially if crucified vertically. The Roman soldiers were trained and experienced at their work.

John, author of the Fourth Gospel, was present when Jesus breathed his last breath. He gives eyewitness testimony that Jesus was truly dead (John 21:24; 19:35). The body of Jesus remained on the cross until the centurion of the execution squad had come to the prefect, Pontius Pilate and convinced him that Jesus was dead. The prefect released the body for burial only upon the centurion's assurances that Jesus was indeed dead. This was no mere formality in the case of Jesus. The brevity of the time Jesus had been crucified led the prefect to press the question whether or not he was dead. But the answers of the centurion convinced him.

The 'swoon' theory is based on the supposition that Jesus revived in the tomb and was later released to live out his days in obscurity. This detail is improbable. Even had Jesus not died on the cross he would have died in the tomb without water and medical care.

All the evidence points to Jesus' death on the Friday afternoon.

The body was removed from the tomb

The reason the tomb was empty, it is suggested, is that someone removed the corpse between the time of the burial late on Friday afternoon and the arrival of the women early on Sunday morning.

The strongest factor against this is the presence of the burial cloths in the tomb. Had the body been removed it would not have been unwrapped, so bloodied would it have been.

But who might have done this and why?

Neither Jews nor Romans would have wanted the body to be other than in the tomb, as powerful evidence that the influential messianic pretender was indeed dead. Such was to be the fate of those who create public disturbance against the might of Rome and her Caesar! Both Jews and Romans could point to both the place where he was crucified and the place where he was buried. The bones of Jesus in the tomb in which he was buried would stand as an irrefutable denial of the claims he had made and the hopes that had been invested in him.

In any case, had either Jew or Roman taken the body, they would immediately have produced it when the disciples began to proclaim that Jesus was raised alive.

It was widely believed at the time that the *disciples* had taken the body. But Matthew states that the temple authorities bribed the Roman soldiers to say this (Matt. 28:11–15). Matthew's rebuttal of the widespread belief among the Jews that the disciples had taken the body is clear evidence that the tomb in which Jesus had been buried was empty. Throughout the next two centuries the Jewish counterclaim was that the disciples had taken the body.[26]

The disciples had come armed to Jerusalem expecting a messianic showdown (Acts 1:6; cf. Luke 24:21).[27] They did not expect Jesus to be raised because they did not expect him to be killed. By definition the Messiah was a victor and they had come with him to share in the spoils of his apocalyptic triumph. On the way to Jerusalem, James and John wanted to have places of power when he entered into his glory (Mark 10:35–37). Jesus' words about his death and resurrection as they travelled to Jerusalem were simply not understood (Mark 9:10; 10:32). The report of the women that the tomb

---

26. See Justin Martyr, *Dial.* 108; Tertullian, *Spect.* 30.

27. Luke 22:49–50; cf. Luke 19:11.

was empty and that Jesus' promise that he would be raised the third day had been fulfilled was greeted by the disciples with disbelief as an idle tale (Luke 24:11).

The suggestion, then, that these deeply disappointed men, steeped in apocalyptic hopes, suddenly thought of stealing the body and saying that Jesus, as an individual, had been raised from the dead before the onset of the end of the world is improbable.

The women returned to the wrong tomb

This explanation states that the women made the simplest mistake. They returned to the wrong tomb, found it empty and declared that the Lord had risen.[28]

By the time Jesus had died it was middle to late afternoon; a new day, the Sabbath, would soon begin. With the rapid approach of the Passover Sabbath Jesus had to be taken from the cross and buried, otherwise the land would be defiled (Deut. 21:23; John 19:31, 42).

The records show that Joseph of Arimathea, a member of the Sanhedrin, made his new tomb available for the burial of Jesus (Matt. 27:60). It is clear from the records that Joseph's tomb was close to Golgotha, the site of the crucifixion (John 19:40, 42). Golgotha itself was close to the walls of Jerusalem; the *titulus*, the caption attached to Jesus' cross, could be read from the city wall (John 19:20).

In other words, the tomb was readily locatable, being (1) close to Jesus' cross, which was close to the city walls, and (2) a substantial tomb, belonging to one of the most prominent members of the community.

Each Gospel tells us that the tomb to which the women came, which they found empty, belonged to a man of high profile with whom the story could readily be checked.

Moreover the Gospels indicate that the women had sat opposite the tomb: they had seen 'where' and 'how' the burial had occurred.[29]

---

28. A view associated with K. Lake, *The Historical Evidence for the Resurrection of Jesus* (New York: Putnam, 1907).

29. Matt. 27:61; Mark 15:47; Luke 23:55.

The 'mistaken tomb' explanation is unlikely and goes against the evidence given for the burial of Jesus.

The disciples also came to the tomb on the report of the women (Luke 24:24). The beloved disciple, author of the Fourth Gospel, was one of those who came to the tomb. He testifies as an eyewitness that only Jesus' burial cloths were found in the tomb (John 20:5–8). The presence of burial cloths confirms that the women had, indeed, come to the right place. Clearly they had come to the tomb in which Jesus had been buried.

The resurrection stories are legendary

It is well established that legends take many years, in fact decades and centuries, to develop.[30]

But *the first day of the week* tradition arose from the women who went to the tomb. It became fixed immediately, as the significant day of the week, because from the beginning the disciples began to meet on that day, the first day of the week to commemorate the Lord's resurrection.[31]

The other tradition, that Christ was raised on the *third day*, also became critical in early Christianity. It arose in Jerusalem soon after the resurrection and was embedded in the tradition Paul 'received' (1 Cor. 15:3–8).

These markers – *the first day of the week* and the *on the third day* traditions – arose immediately after the resurrection of Jesus and for no other reason than to describe the reality of what had happened. On *the first day of the week* (Sunday) the tomb was empty because *on the third day* after his crucifixion (Sunday) Jesus had been raised from the dead.

The earliness and sober concreteness of these traditions about the resurrection is quite different from the vague and frequently bizarre notions associated with the evolution of legends.

---

30. See P. R. Eddy and G. Boyd, *The Jesus Legend: A Case for the Historical Reliability of the Synoptic Jesus Tradition* (Grand Rapids: Baker Academic, 2007), pp. 13–35.

31. John 20:26; cf. Acts 20:7; 1 Cor. 16:2.

The resurrection originated in the Osiris myth

Some people argue that the Egyptian myth of Isis and Osiris was the real source of the New Testament proclamation of the resurrection of Jesus. The ancient Egyptian myth of Isis and Osiris, in Hellenized form, became a popular cult around the Mediterranean world in the centuries after Alexander's conquest of Egypt in the fourth century BC.

According to the myth, Osiris, who had been a pharaoh, was murdered and mutilated by his brother Set. Isis, Osiris' sister and wife, collected and buried his remains and caused him to be reanimated as the god of the dead. Thus Osiris reigns over the underworld as a mummy; his 'new life' is a replica of earthly life.

The association of Jesus with Osiris was fashionable in earlier generations, largely through the influence of Sir James Frazer's *The Golden Bough*, published in 1906. The German scholar Rudolph Bultmann advocated a version of the dying and rising god as the explanation of the resurrection of Jesus. Bultmann's supposed parallels, however, all postdate the New Testament by several hundred years.

Few today pursue this line of thought.

We should note that (1) the grotesque story of Isis and Osiris is quite unlike the account of the resurrection of Jesus; (2) as devout Jews, and therefore monotheists, the disciples would have had no part in an idolatrous Gentile cult or its beliefs; (3) the account of Jesus gives people, time and place specifics that, by their nature, are not found in myths, which have no historical basis; (4) the formal credo about the resurrection of Jesus had been established within so brief a period as two or three years of the event (1 Cor. 15:3–7); and (5) Jesus is not a reanimated god over the nether regions; rather he is alive for evermore, the Lord both of the dead and the living (Rev. 1:18; Rom. 14:9).

Summary

We conclude that, when carefully considered, these and related theories are unconvincing. It is striking that those who reject the resurrection of Jesus have not settled on one major objection to the historicity of the resurrection.

Evaluation of the evidence

The analysis of the resurrection belongs to disciplines that evaluate *evidence*, in particular those of the historian and the lawyer. Over the years, however, many noted scientists, as well as historians and lawyers have argued for the resurrection of Jesus based on evidence.

Francis Collins, Head of the Human Genome Project and former atheist, in his book *The Language of God* describes how his pride and sinfulness prevented him from knowing God. However, the weight of historical evidence convinced him of the truth of the crucifixion and resurrection of Jesus and so he became a Christian believer.[32]

Scholars employ various criteria to evaluate the historicity of Jesus' words and deeds. One is the *criterion of multiple attestation*, that is, the evidence of a *number* of *independent* witnesses, a test that is applicable for both historians and trial juries. The gospels and their underlying sources provide a fivefold range of such witnesses,[33] satisfying the requirements of this criterion.

The other is the two-sided *criterion of similarity* (to Jewish culture) *and dissimilarity* (from Jewish culture). The events of the first Easter – the trials, the Roman crucifixion, the urgent removal of the body because of the Sabbath, the pre-burial practices, the rock tomb and the rolling stone and many other details – all authentically cohere with the political, religious and cultural circumstances of Jerusalem at that time ('similarity'). On the other hand, however, whilst the universal resurrection was an article of Jewish faith the resurrection of an *individual* was totally unexpected ('dissimilarity').

---

32. F. Collins, *The Language of God* (New York: Free Press, 2006), pp. 221-223.

33. Mark, John, Q, L, and M witness independently to the resurrection of Jesus.

The information in the Gospels satisfies these criteria.

Reduced to basics, the alternatives are either that one (1) accepts the evidence as true or (2) concludes that the first Christians were mistaken or that they perpetrated an elaborate fraud. But the quality of the evidence and the moral tone of the literature in which it occurs lead many to conclude that Jesus, having been crucified, was, after three days, raised from the dead on the first day of Passover week.

Significance of the resurrection

The case I have been putting is that the worship of Jesus as 'Lord' by the early Christians (a fact) is entirely consistent with his pre-resurrection identity as Messiah, Son of God and Son of Man. The alternative, that Jesus was *only* a prophet or rabbi, leaves unexplained the immediate worship of him post-resurrection. Rather his supra-natural identity, powerful mission and miracles find a logical continuity after his death as one proclaimed and venerated as the exalted Lord.

What was the role of the resurrection in this? In my view, the resurrection confirmed Jesus' pre-resurrection identity and mission as Messiah. It did not, however, make him into something he had not been beforehand.

11. OTHER GOSPELS?

On the day called Sunday . . . the memoirs of the apostles [the Gospels]
are read as long as time permits.

Justin Martyr

The New Atheists assert that the canonical Gospels were chosen
arbitrarily from a wider selection of competitors.[1] Hitchens even
asserts that these Gnostic Gospels were 'of the same period and
provenance as many of the subsequently canonical and "authorized"
Gospels'.[2]

The existence of gospels other than the four canonical ones
has been known for many years. Until recent times these have
been regarded as 'curiosities' from later centuries, having little
claim to represent the life and teachings of the historical Jesus
authentically.

---

1. R. Dawkins, *The God Delusion* (London: Bantam, 2006), p. 95.
2. C. Hitchens, *God Is Not Great: How Religion Poisons Everything* (New
   York: Twelve, 2007), pp. 112–113.

Two classes of reference

Allusions

There are two classes of reference. First, the Church Fathers allude to gospels for which we have little or no direct evidence, that is, the *Gospel of the Ebionites* (Irenaeus, *Haer.* 1.26.2; 3.21.1), the *Gospel of the Nazoreans* (Eusebius, *Hist. eccl.* 4.22.8), the *Gospel of the Hebrews* (Clement of Alexandria, *Strom.* 2.9.45).

In the absence of passages from these texts we can do little more than speculate as to their origin or character. These works appear to have been compiled for Jewish Christians who remained outside mainstream Gentile Christianity (known as Ebionites and Nazoreans), and who seem to have continued Jewish practices (circumcision, Sabbath, the religious calendar).[3] There are hints in the Church Fathers that these gospels are adaptations of Matthew (as the most 'Jewish' of the Gospels).

Surviving texts

The second category consists of surviving texts such as Valentinus' *Gospel of Truth*, an *Unknown Gospel*, the *Gospel of Peter* and the *Gospel of Thomas*. These are the 'Gnostic Gospels' that Dawkins and Hitchens think are of equal value with the four Gospels, that is, of little or no value!

One such text is Valentinus' *Gospel of Truth*, which is not really a gospel since there is no narrative whatsoever. Furthermore it is obviously derived from a pastiche of texts from the New Testament.

The *Unknown Gospel* (*P. Egerton* 2) is an important text confidently dated to the middle of the second century AD.[4] It consists of several short fragments of broken text. It is cast in narrative form, so that it can be called a 'gospel'. It has connections with the canonical

---

3. See J. E. Taylor, 'The Phenomenon of Early Jewish-Christianity: Reality or Scholarly Invention?', *VC* 44 (1990), pp. 313–334.

4. H. I. Bell and T. C. Skeat, *Fragments of an Unknown Gospel and Other Early Christian Papyri* (London: British Museum, 1935).

Gospels (including John's), and perhaps with the *Infancy Gospel of Thomas* (a different work to the *Gospel of Thomas*). It is free of any explicitly heretical doctrine and lacks the exaggerations found in other second-century works such as the *Gospel of Peter*.

The major issue, of course, is whether it is a source or redaction of the canonical Gospels.[5] The careful observation of E. C. Colwell should be noted: 'the new evangelist had read the four-fold gospel more than once and uses it as a source for his own work'.[6] The fragmentary remains of this *Unknown Gospel* most likely attest an early attempt at creating a gospel harmony, anticipating the efforts of Justin Martyr who created expanses of harmonized texts drawn from the canonical Gospels. These, in turn, anticipated a full-scale harmony, the *Diatessaron* of Justin's pupil Tatian.[7]

The *Gospel of Peter* is a second-century work cast in a narrative format, chiefly related to the passion and resurrection of Christ. Although some have argued that (an earlier version of) the *Gospel of Peter* was a source of the Synoptic Gospels,[8] the reverse is more likely.[9] Peter Head concludes, 'The cumulative evidence for a second century date is strong and adds to the impression that the *Gospel of Peter* is a redaction of the canonical material (perhaps also influenced by oral traditions).'[10]

---

5. Bell and Skeat (ibid., pp. 26–29) believe this text may be a source for the Gospel of John. See also H. Koester, 'Apocryphal and Canonical Gospels', *HTR* 73.12 (1980), pp. 105–130, who is more emphatic that it 'preserves features which derive from a stage of the tradition that is older than the canonical Gospels' (p. 120). For a contrary view see C. A. Evans, *Fabricating Jesus* (Downers Grove: InterVarsity Press, 2007), pp. 85–92.

6. E. C. Colwell, Review of Bell and Skeat, *Unknown Gospel*, in *JR* 16.4 (1936), pp. 478–480.

7. See further Evans, *Fabricating Jesus*, p. 89.

8. So P. A. Mirecki, 'Peter, Gospel of', in *ABD* 5.278–281.

9. P. M. Head, 'On the Christology of the Gospel of Peter', *VC* 46.3 (1992), pp. 209–224.

10. Ibid., p. 218.

The *Gospel of Thomas* does not belong to the gospel genre since it is not a narrative but a series of sayings of Jesus. It is a fourth-century Coptic text that appears to have been translated from a second-century Greek version (a view supported by Greek papyri fragments *P. Oxyrynchus* 654, I, 655). The *Gospel of Thomas* is not a straight translation since in the intervening century the Coptic version seems to have assimilated to the Coptic version of the New Testament. Consequently we cannot confidently retrovert the Coptic version back to a second-century Greek original. In effect, we are left with the fourth-century version.

There are many sayings that bear close similarity to sayings of Jesus in the Synoptic Gospels. So the burning question is, 'Did the *Gospel of Thomas* depend on the Gospels, or was it written independently of them?' The issue is complex and scholars are divided. One complication is that the *Gospel of Thomas* may have borrowed from a now-lost gospel (e.g. the *Gospel of the Hebrews*).

The main argument for the independence of the *Gospel of Thomas* is that its order differs from the Gospels. If it is dependent, so the argument runs, why does it change the Synoptic Gospels' order? Furthermore the sequence of the Coptic *Gospel of Thomas* appears to follow an idiosyncratic structure as dictated by link words.

In respect of the dependency argument, C. Tuckett has pointed to a number of passages where the *Gospel of Thomas* appears to depend on finished (i.e. redacted) versions of the Synoptics,[11] for example, 5 ('there is nothing hidden that will not be manifest'), 9 (parable of the sower), 16 ('I have come to throw divisions upon the earth'), 20 (parable of mustard seed), 55 ('Whoever does not hate father and mother'). Tuckett does not 'deduce . . . that *Gospel of Thomas* is dependent on the synoptics *in toto*';[12] he finds that the texts he has reviewed point in that direction.

---

11. C. Tuckett, 'Thomas and the Synoptics', *NovT* 30.7 (1988), pp. 132–157; 'Synoptic Traditions in Some Nag Hammadi and Related Texts', *VC* 36 (1982), pp. 173–190.

12. Ibid., p. 188.

A second consideration noted by Tuckett is that the parable of the sower in the *Gospel of Thomas* is a 'gnosticising redaction of the synoptic parable'.[13] In other words, at this point at least the *Gospel of Thomas* reflects a Gnostic origin in the second century or later. J. H. Wood found that the *Gospel of Thomas* has many points of contact with other second-century texts that reveal dependence on the canonical Gospels.[14] Wood argues for the reliance of the *Gospel of Thomas* on all four Gospels, and therefore that it is an early witness to the fourfold gospel (see table 11.1 below).

Table 11.1 Parallels between the Gospels of Matthew, Luke and John and the *Gospel of Thomas*

Matthew	Thomas	Luke	Thomas	John	Thomas
5:10	69a	11:27–28	79	1:9	24
5:14	32	12:13–14	72	1:14	28
6:2–4	6, 14	12:16–21	63	4:13–15	13
6:3	62	12:49	10	7:32–36	38
7:6	93	17:20–21	3	8:12; 9:5	77
10:16	39				
11:30	90				
13:24–30	57				
13:44	109				
13:45–46	76				
13:47–50	8				
15:13	40				
18:20	30				
23:13	39, 102				

Who is depending on whom, the above three Gospels on *Thomas*, or *Thomas* on the above three? For two reasons at least we conclude

13. Ibid., p. 189.
14. J. H. Wood, Jr., 'The New Testament Gospels and the Gospel of Thomas: A New Direction', *NTS* 52 (2005), pp. 579–595.

that *Thomas* is depending on Matthew, Luke and John. The first is that *Thomas* does not follow the sequence of Matthew, Luke or John (which more or less follow the same sequence) but has diverged dramatically from each. It is more likely that *Thomas* has selected sayings of Jesus from the above three according to its predetermined sequence than that the three each 'scrambled' *Thomas*'s sequence. The second is *Thomas*'s identifiable tendency to infuse second-century Gnostic 'colour' into the non-Gnostic words of Jesus in Matthew, Luke and John. It is most likely, therefore, that the *Gospel of Thomas* is a later work based on selected parts of three extant Gospels: Matthew, Luke and John.

While some have hoped that the *Gospel of Thomas* would prove to predate the canonical Gospels and to reveal new information about Jesus, the evidence points rather to the significance of this text as a window into *second-century* Gnostic Christianity. In any case, it is a late Coptic text whose connections with its second-century Greek antecedent remain problematic (see fig. 11.1 below for approximate dates of the non-canonical gospels).

120	150	160	180
Gospel of Nazoreans	*P. Egerton 2*	*Gospel of*	*Gospel of*
Gospel of the Ebionites	*Gospel of Truth?*	*Peter*	*Thomas*

Fig. 11.1 Dates of second-century gospels (approximate).

To summarize, the 'other' gospels accessible to us – the *Gospel of the Nazoreans*, the *Gospel of the Ebionites*, the *Gospel of Truth*, the *Gospel of Peter*, the *Unknown Gospel* (*P. Egerton 2*) and the *Gospel of Thomas* – all prove to be of second-century origin. In each case their similarities with the canonical Gospels is best explained by their dependency on them. Whereas the *Gospel of the Nazoreans*, the *Gospel of the Ebionites* and the *Unknown Gospel* generally reproduce Matthew with a markedly Jewish interest, the *Gospel of Peter* appears to be a Gnosticized version of Mark. The *Gospel of Truth* and the *Gospel of Thomas* are not cast as narratives and should not be called 'gospels'.[15] We are able to eliminate each of these as primary sources of information for the works of the historical Christ. It is possible that some genuine words of Jesus have survived in the *Gospel of Thomas*, though with Gnostic overtones.

The four Gospels belong to the first century

There are three principle reasons for locating the four Gospels in the first century (see chapter 12). The first is that Christian leaders in the second century refer to them, for example Papias (writing *c.* 110–130), who refers specifically to Mark and Matthew and implicitly to Luke and John. Secondly, writers from the second century quote, echo or allude to passages from Matthew, Luke and John. One leader, Tatian, created the *Diatessaron*, a single gospel by combining the four Gospels into one. Thirdly, there are fragments of Gospel texts from early in the second century, including P[52] (from John 18).

We conclude that the four Gospels belong to the first century and that they are the only 'gospels' that qualify for this early dating. The implications of this are considerable, chiefly that the four Gospels were in use in the churches within six decades of Jesus.

Closeness of the Gospels to Jesus

It is important to notice the chronological closeness of the available sources to Jesus, the subject of their biographies.[16]

---

15. For a generally negative assessment of the value of the apocryphal gospels see J. H. Charlesworth and C. A. Evans, 'Jesus in the Agrapha and Apocryphal Gospels', in B. Chilton and C. A. Evans (eds.), *Studying the Historical Jesus* (Leiden: Brill, 1994), pp. 479–533.

16. N. T. Wright, *The New Testament and the People of God* (London: SPCK, 1992), attempted to establish 'fixed points . . . landmarks in the reconstruction of the first century or so of the Christian church' (p. 370).

It is instructive, for example, to compare the sources for Jesus and Tiberius Caesar, under whom Jesus was executed. Both men died within a few years of each other, Jesus in 33 and Tiberius in 37. For Jesus the available sources (the twenty-seven texts of the New Testament) are both numerous and chronologically close to him, whereas for Tiberius the main literary sources (Tacitus, Suetonius and Dio) are relatively fewer and considerably later.[17]

The main reason for the difference is that Jesus became the object of a continuing and growing movement that preserved the key texts by their use of them. Tacitus comments that, notwithstanding the death of 'the founder of the name [Christian]', the 'pernicious super-stition (*superstitio*[18]) . . . *broke out once more*, not only in Judaea . . . but in the capital itself'.[19] Within three decades of the execution of the 'founder' the movement was not only surviving but had also become numerically 'vast' in Rome.

This movement, like the Judaism from which it was an outgrowth, was *text* dependent. The gatherings of the movement were charac-terized by members *reading* texts to one another.[20] Within fifteen years of Jesus' lifespan the first texts (Paul's letters to his mission groups) began appearing. Within thirty-five years of Jesus a biography (Mark's) for church reading (Mark 13:14) appeared, which was soon to be followed by two others (Matthew's and Luke's) based on the earlier version, Mark. The literary sources for Tiberius were

---

17. Tacitus, *Annals* (bks. 1–4), written after 115; Suetonius, *Lives of the Caesars*, written after 120; Dio Cassius' Roman history written *c.* 210. Velleius Paterculus was a contemporary of Tiberius, but his *History of Rome* is fragmentary in character and overly adulatory of Tiberius.

18. *Superstitio* does not mean 'superstition' in the modern sense. Rather Roman writers used it to portray a foreign cult whose core beliefs were inimical to the Roman state. See L. F. Janssen, '"Superstitio" and the Persecution of the Christians', *VC* 33 (1979), pp. 131–159.

19. Tacitus, *Annals of Imperial Rome*, tr. M. Grant (Harmondsworth: Penguin Classics, 1985), 15.44, italics added.

20. See e.g. Mark 13:14; 2 Cor. 1:13; Eph. 3:4; Col. 4:16; 1 Thess. 5:27; Rev. 1:3.

written due to Roman concern to document their past, whereas the sources for Jesus, the Gospels, were written to provide texts for *current* church-based instruction and worship, based on the conviction that he was a living contemporary ('Lord'). This, above all, accounts for the frequency and earliness of the texts about Jesus.

The phenomenon of chronological closeness of these sources to their subject, Jesus, is noteworthy. In terms of the documentation of key figures in antiquity this is a phenomenon almost without parallel. The letters of Paul and others are earlier still and begin to appear within a decade and a half of the first Easter.

Equally noteworthy is the literary ingenuity reflected in this gospel literature. Most scholars agree that the Gospels, while resembling biographies of the period, are nonetheless innovative, in effect pioneering a new genre. Recent scholarship has commented on significant levels of literary sophistication evident within these texts (e.g. their engagement with the implied readers[21]). Yet the literary development in the three Synoptic texts occurred from first to last over a period as brief as twenty years.

---

21. For the Gospel of Mark see e.g. P. G. Bolt, 'Mark's Gospel', in S. McKnight and G. R. Osborne (eds.), *The Face of New Testament Studies* (Grand Rapids: Baker, 2004), pp. 396–405; for the Gospel of Matthew, e.g. D. Senior, *The Gospel of Matthew* (Nashville: Abingdon, 1997); D. C. Allison, *Studies in Matthew* (Grand Rapids: Baker Academic, 2005), pp. 135–155.

12. THE TRANSMISSION IS TRUSTWORTHY

It is reassuring . . . to find that the general result of all these discoveries and all this study is to strengthen the proof of the authenticity of the Scriptures, and our conviction that we have in our hands, in substantial integrity, the veritable Word of God.

Sir Frederick Kenyon

The New Atheists identify two areas of unreliable transmission. The first is the unreliable oral history of the gospel tradition. They liken this to 'Chinese whispers',[1] involving 'hearsay upon hearsay'.[2] To Hitchens this helps explain the contradictions between the Gospels.[3]

The second is unreliable textual transmission. They claim the Gospels, once written, were 'recopied through fallible scribes'.[4] Harris suggests the texts 'have not retained their integrity over time'.[5] Hitchens suggests the New Testament shows 'unmistakable signs of having been tampered with'.[6]

---

1. R. Dawkins, *The God Delusion* (London: Bantam, 2006), p. 93.
2. C. Hitchens, *God Is Not Great: How Religion Poisons Everything* (New York: Twelve, 2007), p. 120.
3. Ibid.
4. Dawkins, *God Delusion*, p. 93.
5. S. Harris, *The End of Faith: Religion, Terror and the Future of Reason* (New York: Norton, 2004), p. 20.
6. Hitchens, *God Is Not Great*, p. 110.

The New Atheists also share a common interest in the work and story of Bart Ehrman.[7] They recommend or quote his *Misquoting Jesus*,[8] and outline his journey from 'Bible-believing fundamentalist to thoughtful sceptic',[9] who 'could not reconcile his faith with his scholarship'.[10] Moreover they suggest that Ehrman has exposed the 'huge uncertainty befogging the New Testament texts'.[11] Perceived unreliable textual transmission is compounded by the suggestion that the documents were written long after the purported events.[12]

These are serious challenges to gospel truth. If the words in our Bibles have not been transmitted accurately how can we believe them?

Chronology

The first step in a response to these claims is to establish a chronology for the writing of the Gospels in relationship with the lifespan of Jesus. Scholars agree (1) that the first Easter is to be dated to AD 33 (or 30), (2) that the earliest Gospel, Mark, was written before AD 70, and (3) that the other Gospels were written within a decade or so of Mark (see fig. 12.1 below). Small variations in dating points 1, 2 and 3 do not affect this discussion.

28–33	33–65	65–80	95–150
Jesus	Formation of gospel traditions	Writing of Gospels	Post-apostolic writing

Fig. 12.1 Timeline: through the formation of the gospel tradition to the post-apostolic witness.

---

7. B. D. Ehrman, *Misquoting Jesus: The Story of Who Changed the Bible and Why* (San Francisco: HarperSanFrancisco, 2005).

8. Dawkins, *God Delusion*, p. 95; Hitchens, *God Is Not Great*, pp. 120–122.

9. Dawkins, *God Delusion*, p. 95.

10. Hitchens, *God Is Not Great*, p. 120.

11. Ibid., p. 95.

12. Hitchens, *God Is Not Great*, pp. 110–111, 143.

What is important, however, is to recognize what was happening in the thirty or so years between Jesus and the writing of Mark and the other Gospels. Jesus, through his original disciples, created a movement and a mission. That movement created teaching resources for the churches by means of memorized teachings and written teachings. The Gospels were the final, 'written-up' versions of those oral and written traditions.

Thus the 'space' between Jesus and the Gospels was not empty but 'alive' with missionary activity. Furthermore it is a relatively short period. At the time of writing, this author had been married almost fifty years, and was an ordained minister for the same period. He easily recalls the major events within a time frame that is longer than that separating the writing of Mark from Jesus.

Through the Acts of the Apostles, which covers the thirty years after Jesus, and from the letters of Paul, James, Peter and the letter to the Hebrews within that thirty-year period we see the leaders preaching the gospel, people turning to the Lord and the formation of congregations of Christians. This explosive movement needed resources for these congregations, and the leaders provided these as oral and written resources. These 'traditions' were focused on Jesus – what he *said* and *did*, what *happened* to him, and what he *achieved*.

Traditions – oral and written

The teachings *of* Jesus and *about* Jesus were transmitted by two modes, oral and written.

Oral tradition

Oral transmission of teaching was significant within Jewish culture in the era of Jesus (cf. Mark 7:3, 9–13; Gal. 1:13–14). Since Jesus and the disciples were Jews, it is no surprise that there are many evidences of oral transmission of teaching in the New Testament.

Paul commends the Corinthians because 'you . . . maintain the *traditions* even as I *delivered them* to you' (1 Cor. 11:2), for example, the 'tradition' of the Last/Lord's Supper and the 'tradition' of the death, burial and resurrection of the Christ (1 Cor. 11:23; 15:1–3). Believers are those who have 'learned Christ', that is, who have 'heard' and 'been taught' and who are now 'walking' according to Christ (Eph. 4:20–21; cf. 1:13; 1 Thess. 4:1). This is a new 'way to live' as 'received' from Christ, 'handed over' by Paul and 'received' by believers.

Paul is thankful that the Christians in Rome 'have become obedient from the heart to the *pattern* of teaching' to which they had been "handed over"' (Rom. 6:17, my tr.). This implies that Christians in Rome had been orally catechized prior to baptism. At the end of the letter Paul warns the Romans to take note of those who oppose 'the teaching' they have 'learned' (Rom. 16:17).

Luke also refers to this technical 'rabbinic' vocabulary as the 'apostles' teaching' in the early church in Jerusalem (Acts 2:42; 5:28). The readers of the letter to the Hebrews, having 'heard' the living word of God, ought by now to be *teachers* of others (Heb. 4:2, 12–13; 5:11–12; 6:1). Prominent also in Hebrews is the notion of a 'confession', a body of teaching the readers were to 'consider' and 'hold to' (Heb. 3:1; 4:13; 10:23). John's second letter speaks of 'the doctrine of Christ'. A person who comes from outside is not to be received, unless he brings that 'doctrine' (2 John 9–10). Jude urges his readers to struggle for 'the faith' that was once 'handed over' to the saints (Jude 3). Notice that it is *the* faith, once 'handed over' – rabbi-like – by Jesus to his original followers for which Jude's readers were to contend.

It is almost certain that the pattern of oral teaching begun by Jesus continued after Easter and became a feature of early Christianity for a century or more. There is the well-known reference by Papias (AD 130) to his preference for the 'living voice' over 'books'. The oral transmission evident in 'Rabbi' Jesus' method of rote teaching, as continued by his disciples after Easter, was *didactic*, transmitted authoritatively and by rote from teacher to disciple.

The New Atheists claim that this oral tradition was unreliable and subject to distortion. The truth is otherwise. The rabbis were careful

to memorize exactly the words of their teachers, which they transmitted exactly to their disciples. 'Rabbi' Jesus and 'Rabbi' Paul
and the other Jewish leaders belonged to a culture where precise
memorization and verbatim transmission were the norm.

Written tradition

At the same time, however, *written* traditions existed side by side with
oral traditions in the world of Jewish Christianity in the three or so
decades between Jesus and the Gospel of Mark.[13] The study of the
Dead Sea Scrolls has revealed a strong writing culture that existed
side by side with an oral culture.

The opening lines of Luke-Acts tell us that written traditions had
been created within those first decades of Christianity. Luke states
that 'many have undertaken to compile a *narrative* of the things that
have been accomplished among us' (Luke 1:1), that is, *about Jesus*
before and after his resurrection (cf. Acts 1:1–2, 'In the first book
. . . I have dealt with all that Jesus *began* to do and teach, until the day
when he was taken up'). The original disciples 'delivered' texts to
Luke, amongst them the Gospel of Mark. Luke based his Gospel
on the Gospel of Mark, to which he added other written source
material.

The New Atheists accuse the early Christians of distortion and
inaccuracy. Is this true?

In fact it is not. Because Luke uses Mark we are able to check his
accuracy in the use he makes of Mark. Does Luke embellish Mark?
Does he make a 'god' out of Jesus, a mere man? Does he exaggerate
or mislead? Luke does none of these things, as you can easily check
by setting Luke and Mark side by side. What we discover might come
as a surprise. Luke usually *shortens* Mark's text and in no way expands
or heightens the Jesus we find in Mark. Luke abbreviates Mark
because he has other source material to weave into his enlarged

---

13. On the dynamic relationship between the oral and the written see J. D.
Harvey, 'Orality and Its Implications for Biblical Studies: Recapturing
an Ancient Paradigm', *JETS* 45.1 (2002), pp. 99–109.

Gospel, for example, his nativity narrative and great parables such as the prodigal son. As we cross-check Luke against Mark we find that Luke is a careful and credible copyist. Luke is no merely passive copyist, however, but a writer who infuses texts he has received with his own insights.

Matthew also uses Mark's Gospel and reproduces about 90% of his Gospel. As with Luke, Matthew follows Mark's sequence and closely reproduces his text. Does Matthew 'beef up' Mark's Jesus? As with Luke, the answer is, 'No, he does not.'

John writes independently of the other three, so that we cannot put John alongside Mark in the same way as with Luke and Matthew. But John follows the same overall historical and geographical sequence as Mark, Luke and Matthew. As well, there are a number of passages that narrate the same events, for example, the feeding of the multitude or Jesus' Palm Sunday arrival into Jerusalem. John brings out different emphases, but the events are the same.[14]

Letter writing

Paul's earliest letters, such as Galatians and 1 Thessalonians, written between AD 48 and 50, are so well formed stylistically that it suggests these were not his first written texts. Paul may have written earlier letters (from the early forties?) that have not survived. In other words, from early times the Christian leaders employed letter writing in the course of their missionary work.

Thus the few decades between Jesus and the first writing of the Gospels (*c.* 33–65) were characterized by the writing of letters – by Paul, James, Peter, the writer to the Hebrews and the Jerusalem Council. John's letters including Revelation (a letter-book) were written later, after the period in which the Gospels of Matthew, Luke and John were written.

---

14. See P. W. Barnett, *Finding the Historical Christ* (Grand Rapids: Eerdmans, 2009), pp. 147–155.

Gospel traditions in the letters

Paul's letters

Paul's letters contain echoes of the 'instructions' of the Lord. Echoes of the teaching of Jesus can be heard in at least three letters of Paul, each of which is datable. They are 1 Thessalonians (AD 50), 1 Corinthians (AD 55) and Romans (AD 57).

1 Thessalonians In 1 Thessalonians 4:13 – 5:11 Paul echoes teachings of Jesus drawn from various sources that later formed part of the written Gospels (see table 12.1 below).[15]

In common between Paul's passage in 1 Thessalonians and Jesus' end-time teaching in the Gospels are (1) the sudden appearance of the Lord, as in the parable of the thief, (2) the trumpet call signalling the gathering of the elect, and (3) the warning for watchfulness, as in the parable of sleeping and waking. The connections, though evocative, are real.

Table 12.1 1 Thessalonians and the Jesus tradition

1 Thessalonians	*The Jesus tradition*
4:15–16 'For this we declare to you by a word from the Lord, that we who are alive, who are left until the coming of the Lord, will not precede those who have fallen asleep. For the Lord himself will descend from heaven with a cry of command, with the voice of an archangel, and with the sound of the *trumpet* of God. And the dead in Christ will arise first.'	Matt. 24:31 'he will send out his angels with a loud *trumpet* call, and they will gather his elect from the four winds'

15. See S. Kim, 'The Jesus Tradition in 1Thess 4:13–5:11', *NTS* 48 (2002), pp. 225–242.

1 Thessalonians	*The Jesus tradition*
5:2–6 'For you yourselves are fully aware that the day of the Lord will come like a *thief* in the night. While people are saying, "There is peace and security," then sudden destruction will come upon them as labour pains come upon a pregnant woman, and they will not escape. But you are not in darkness, brothers, for that day to surprise you like a *thief*. For you are all children of light, children of the day. We are not of the night or of the darkness. So then let us not sleep, as others do, but let us keep *awake* and be sober.'	Matt. 24:42–43 'Therefore, stay awake, for you do not know on what day your Lord is coming. But know this, that if the master of the house had known in what part of the night the *thief* was coming, he would have stayed awake and would not have let his house be broken into.' Luke 21:34–36 'But watch yourselves lest your hearts be weighed down with dissipation and drunkenness . . . and that day come upon you suddenly like a trap . . . But *stay awake* at all times, praying that you may have strength to escape all these things that are going to take place, and to stand before the Son of Man.'

As well, it is likely Paul's appeal to sexual holiness springs from Jesus' injunction about the permanence of marriage (1 Thess. 4:1–8; Mark 10:9). Paul calls this 'instructions' he gave 'through the Lord Jesus' (1 Thess. 4:2). There are also allusions to Jesus' teachings elsewhere in the letter, for example, 'Be at peace among yourselves' (5:13; cf. Mark 9:50), and 'See that no one repays anyone evil for evil' (5:15; cf. Matt. 5:38–48).

1 Corinthians There are three occasions in 1 Corinthians where Paul refers explicitly to a 'charge' or command of 'the Lord' (see table 12.2 opposite).

By the time Paul wrote 1 Corinthians in the mid-fifties, various teachings of the Lord were current, probably in written form.

Romans The 'ethical' section of Romans (chs. 12–14) has a number of allusions to teachings of Jesus as found in the source Matthew

Table 12.2 1 Corinthians and the Jesus tradition

Paul in 1 Corinthians	The Jesus tradition
7:10–11 'To the married I give this charge (not I, but the Lord): the wife should not separate from her husband (but if she does, she should remain unmarried or else be reconciled to her husband), and the husband should not divorce his wife.'	Mark 10:9, 11–12 (cf. Luke 16:18; Matt. 5:32) 'What therefore God has joined together, let not man separate ... Whoever divorces his wife and marries another commits adultery against her, and if she divorces her husband and marries another, she commits adultery.'
9:14 'In the same way, the Lord commanded that those who proclaim the gospel should get their living by the gospel.'[16]	Luke 10:7 / Matt. 10:10 'for the labourer deserves his wages the labourer deserves his food'
11:23–25 'the Lord Jesus on the night when he was betrayed took bread, and when he had given thanks, he broke it, and said, "This is my body which is for you. Do this in remembrance of me."'	Luke 22:19–20 'And he took bread, and when he had given thanks, he broke it and gave it to them, saying, "This is my body, which is given for you. Do this in remembrance of me."' Etc.

and Luke employ (Q). Paul also repeats teachings of Jesus found only in Mark (see table 12.3 on p. 174).

Since the dating of Romans is not in doubt (AD 57) we conclude that the information Paul echoes was current at the time he wrote. This means that the *traditions* set out in Mark, Matthew and Luke were in circulation by the mid-fifties, and probably earlier.

---

16. According to D. C. Allison, 'The Pauline Epistles and the Synoptic Gospels', NTS 28 (1982), p. 13, 'there is adequate ground to claim that Paul had received some version of Jesus' instructions on mission'. See also E. E. Ellis, 'Traditions in 1 Corinthians', NTS 32 (1986), pp. 481–502.

Table 12.3 Romans and the Jesus tradition

Paul in Romans	*Jesus in the Gospels*
12:14 'Bless those who persecute you; bless and do not curse them.'	Luke 6:28 / Matt. 5:44 (Q) 'bless those who curse you, pray for those who abuse you'
12:17 'Repay no one evil for evil.'	Luke 6:27 / Matt. 5:38–48 (Q) 'Love your enemies, do good to those who hate you.'
13:7 'Pay to all what is owed to them.'	Mark 12:17 'Render to Caesar the things that are Caesar's.'
13:8 'the one who loves another has fulfilled the law'	Mark 12:31 'Love your neighbour as yourself.'
14:13 'never put a . . . stumbling block . . . in the way of a brother'	Mark 9:42 'Whoever causes one of these little ones who believe in me to sin.'
14:14 'nothing is unclean in itself'	Mark 7:15 'nothing outside a person . . . can defile him'
14:20 'everything is . . . clean'	Mark 7:19 'Thus [Jesus] declared all foods clean.'

Paul's letters and the teachings of Jesus It is clear that by the time Paul's earliest surviving letters appear in AD 50, collections of Jesus teachings were in circulation. The teachings of the Lord had begun to be assembled some time beforehand, even though we do not know precisely when or from whom Paul received them. Paul's several visits to Jerusalem in the forties would have provided opportunity to obtain this material (Gal. 2:1 / Acts 11:29–30; Acts 15:2).

Paul's letters between AD 50 and 57 (to the Thessalonians, the Corinthians and the Romans) contain direct references to bodies of Jesus' teaching that had by then been collected. While the precise contents of these collections are not known, their existence is certain. By the time the Gospels came to be written there was an established tradition of collecting and passing on the teachings of

the Lord. Echoes of Jesus' teachings found in Paul's letters is historically secure evidence of this.

The letter of James

There are good reasons to believe the letter came from James in
Jerusalem to Christian Jews of the Diaspora. But when was it written?
It is an early letter written from the time of James's leadership of the
church in Jerusalem (from AD 41) and prior to his death in AD 62.

The letter of James has many allusions to the Jesus tradition.

First, there are numerous words in common between Matthew
and James, for example, 'perfect' (Jas 1:4; Matt. 5:48; 19:21), 'righteousness' (Jas 1:20; 3:18; Matt. 3:15; 5:6, 10, 20; 6:1, 33), 'church'
(Jas 5:7; Matt. 16:18; 18:17), 'parousia' (Jas 5:7; Matt. 24:3, 27, 37,
39), 'oaths' (Jas 5:12; Matt. 5:33–37).[17]

Secondly, James makes many textual allusions to the teaching of
Jesus, mostly from traditions later embedded in Matthew and Luke
(see table 12.4 on pp. 176–179).

The amount of James's teaching cross-referenced in the sources
of Matthew and Luke is impressive. It is noteworthy, however, that
James does not attribute this teaching to Jesus. Jesus' teaching has
become James's teaching. The same holds true for allusions in 1 Peter
that can be traced to the Synoptic sources.[18]

1 Peter

As with the letters of Paul and James we find echoes of Jesus' teachings
that will later be incorporated in the Gospels (see table 12.5 on p. 180).[19]

---

17. For a complete list see J. B. Adamson, *The Epistle of James*, NICNT
   (Grand Rapids: Eerdmans, 1976), p. 188.
18. See e.g. E. G. Selwyn, *The First Epistle of Peter* (London: Macmillan,
   1961), pp. 23–24.
19. See R. H. Gundry, '"Verba Christi" in 1 Peter: Their Implications
   Concerning the Authorship of 1 Peter and the Authorship of the
   Gospel Tradition', *NTS* 13 (1966–7), pp. 336–359; 'Further Verba
   on the Verba Christi in First Peter', *Bib* 55 (1974), pp. 211–232. For
   a contra view see E. Best, *1 Peter*, NCB (London: Oliphants, 1971).

Table 12.4 James and the Jesus tradition

James	Matthew	Luke
1:2 'Count it all joy . . . when you meet trials of various kinds.'	5:10, 12 'Blessed are those who are persecuted . . . '	
1:12 'Blessed is the man who remains steadfast under trial.'	'Rejoice and be glad . . . '	
1:5 'If any of you lacks wisdom, let him ask God, who gives generously to all . . . '	7:7 'Ask, and it will be given to you.'	11:9 'ask, and it will be given to you'
1:17 'Every good gift . . . coming down from the Father . . . '	7:11 'how much more will your Father . . . give good things to those who ask him!'	11:13 'how much more will the heavenly Father give the Holy Spirit to those who ask him!'
1:20 'the anger of man does not produce the righteousness of God'	5:22 'everyone who is angry with his brother shall be liable to judgment'	
1:22 'be doers of the word, and not hearers only'	7:24 'Everyone then who hears these words of mine . . . and does them . . . '	
2:5 'has not God chosen those who are poor in the world to be . . . heirs of the kingdom'	5:3 'Blessed are the poor in spirit, for theirs is the kingdom of heaven.'	6:20 'Blessed are you who are poor, for yours is the kingdom of God.'
2:8 'the royal law . . . "You shall love your neighbour as yourself"'	22:39 'And a second is like it: "You shall love your neighbour as yourself"' = Mark 12:31	10:27 'You shall love . . . your neighbour as yourself.'

2:10 'Whoever keeps the whole law but fails in one point has become accountable for all of it.'	5:19 'whoever relaxes one of the least of these commandments . . . will be called least in the kingdom of heaven, but whoever does them . . . will be called great in the kingdom'	
2:13 'For judgment is without mercy to one who has shown no mercy. Mercy triumphs over judgment.'	5:7 'Blessed are the merciful, for they shall receive mercy.'	6:37 'forgive, and you will be forgiven'
2:14 'What good is it . . . if someone says he has faith but does not have works . . . ?'	7:21 'Not everyone who says to me, "Lord, Lord," will enter the kingdom of heaven, but the one who does the will of my Father . . .'	6:46 'Why do you call me "Lord, Lord", and not do what I tell you?'
3:12 'Can a fig tree . . . bear olives, or a grapevine produce figs?'	7:16 'Are grapes gathered from thorn bushes, or figs from thorn bushes?'	6:44 'figs are not gathered from thorn bushes, nor are grapes picked from a bramble bush'
3:13 'Who is wise and understanding among you? By his good conduct let him show his works in the meekness of wisdom.'	5:5 'Blessed are the meek . . .'	
4:4 'Do you not know that friendship with the world is enmity with God? Therefore whoever wishes to be a friend of the world makes himself an enemy of God.'	6:24 'No one can serve two masters, for either he will hate the one and love the other, or he will be devoted to the one and despise the other. You cannot serve God and money.'	16:13 'No servant can serve two masters, for either he will hate the one and love the other, or he will be devoted to the one and despise the other. You cannot serve God and money.'

James	Matthew	Luke
4:8 'Cleanse your hands, you sinners, and purify your hearts, you double-minded.'	5:8 'Blessed are the pure in heart, for they shall see God.'	
4:9 'Be wretched and mourn and weep. Let your laughter be turned to mourning and your joy to gloom.'		6:25 'Woe to you who laugh now, for you shall mourn and weep.'
4:10 'Humble yourselves before the Lord, and he will exalt you.'	23:12 'Whoever exalts himself will be humbled, and whoever humbles himself will be exalted.'	14:11 'everyone who exalts himself will be humbled, and he who humbles himself will be exalted'
4:11 'Do not speak evil against one another, brothers. The one who speaks against a brother or judges his brother, speaks evil against the law and judges the law.'	5:22 'everyone who is angry with his brother will be liable to judgment' 7:1 'Judge not, that you be not judged.'	
5:1 'Come now, you rich, weep and howl for the miseries that are coming upon you.'	19:23 'only with difficulty will a rich person enter the kingdom of heaven'	6:24–25 'But woe to you who are rich, for you have received your consolation. Woe to you who are full now, for you shall be hungry.'
5:2 'Your riches have rotted and your garments are moth-eaten.'	6:20 'Lay up for yourselves treasures in heaven, where neither moth nor rust destroys . . .'	

5:12 'Do not swear, either by heaven or by earth or by any other oath, but let your "yes" be yes and your "no" be no, so that you may not fall under condemnation.'

5:19–20 'My brothers, if anyone among you wanders from the truth and someone brings him back, let him know that whoever brings back a sinner from his wandering will save his soul from death and will cover a multitude of sins.'

5:34–35 'Do not take an oath at all, either by heaven, for it is the throne of God, or by the earth, for it is his footstool . . .'

18:15 'If your brother sins against you, go tell him his fault, between you and him alone. If he listens to you, you have gained your brother.'

Table 12.5 Peter and the Jesus tradition

1 Peter	Jesus in the Gospels
2:12 'see your *good deeds* and *glorify* God'	Matt. 5:16 'let your light shine before others, so that they may see your *good works* and give *glory* to your Father who is in heaven'
2:20 'when you . . . are beaten for it'	Matt. 5:39 'if any one slaps you on the right cheek . . . '
3:9 'Do not repay evil for evil . . . '	Luke 6:27 'Do good to those who hate you.'
3:14 'if you should suffer for righteousness' sake, you will be blessed'	Matt. 5:10 'Blessed are those who are persecuted for righteousness' sake . . . '
4:14 'If you are insulted for the name of Christ, you are blessed'	Matt. 5:11 'Blessed are you when others revile you . . . '

It is clear that the tradition underlying the Sermon on the Mount is prominent in 1 Peter. As with the Jesus traditions found in the letters of Paul and James it is likely that Peter drew from traditions that were *written*.

The lack of secure dating prevents firm conclusions being drawn. The words of Christ in this letter (written in the mid-sixties) confirm that such material had been assembled and was in circulation prior to their inclusion in the letters in which they appear.

Summary
The letters of Paul, James and Peter were written over a span of less than twenty years enclosed within the thirty or so years between Jesus and the emergence of the Gospels. These letters contain echoes and allusions to oral or, more probably, written bodies of tradition that were employed in church ministries. These silos of tradition were subsequently embodied in the Gospels.

In other words, there are rational and historical explanations for the appearance of the oral and written traditions about Jesus. Those who followed Jesus believed he was the Messiah, a belief confirmed by his resurrection from the dead. He trained his disciples to be missionaries and following his resurrection commissioned them to take the message about him (the 'gospel') to all the nations of the world. From that time they began to assemble verbal and written accounts of his words and deeds as resources for their ministries. Within three decades these teachings began to be consolidated in the four Gospels. Luke's and Matthew's dependence on Mark's Gospel allow us to cross-check their integrity as writers, and they prove to be entirely credible.

In other words, we are able to explain in natural terms how the Gospels came to be written, even if we do not know all the details. It is worth being reminded that texts had to be laboriously copied, so their dissemination was relatively slow. Furthermore although Luke and Matthew were dependent on Mark and other traditions, they wrote independently of each other. John wrote independently of Mark, Luke and Matthew. Moreover each wrote for different ethnic and cultural audiences. It is no surprise, then, that the contents do not mesh exactly at all points. How could it be otherwise? There is no need to suspect some kind of conspiracy or that these writers were wildly inaccurate.

Transmission of the Gospels after their being written

The New Atheists also argue that the Gospels, once written, were not transmitted accurately, so we do not have reliable access to Jesus and early Christianity. As I will argue, this claim is unsustainable. The New Testament texts, as we have them in our Bibles, are 99% true to the texts written by the original authors. This emerges from three connected realities: (1) early references *to* the Gospels, (2) early references *from* the Gospels, and (3) early manuscripts *of* the Gospels.

Early references to the Gospels

Papias

Papias, Bishop of Hierapolis, writing in the first decades of the second century,[20] explains the origins of two Gospels (without using that word).[21] Papias explains that *Mark* wrote his work based on Peter's 'instruction'. By observing that Mark wrote 'accurately' he implicitly referred to *Luke*, who claimed to have written his Gospel 'accurately' (Luke 1:3). Papias also stated that '*Matthew* compiled his oracles in the Hebrew language'. Furthermore it appears that by giving the name of six disciples in the order they appear in the Gospel of *John* Papias knows that Gospel also.[22] We conclude that Papias referred directly to the origins of the Gospels of Mark and Matthew and indirectly to the Gospels of Luke and John. Based on Papias's information it is reasonable to assert that these Gospels were in circulation and use by the end of the first century at the latest.

Papias depended for his information about Mark's Gospel on John the Elder, who in turn depended for his information on 'the disciples of the Lord'. Papias himself had not heard the original disciples of the Lord but only Aristion, John the Elder and the daughters of Philip the evangelist (cf. Acts 21:8–9),[23] who were his contemporaries in Hierapolis. The point is that the Elder's report to Papias came from 'disciples of the Lord', that is, in the first century, perhaps *c.* 80.

---

20. It is usually assumed that Papias wrote *c.* 130, though some have argued for a date as early as *c.* 110. See P. W. Barnett, *Birth of Christianity: The First Twenty Years* (Grand Rapids: Eerdmans, 2005), p. 159.

21. Reported in Eusebius, *Hist. eccl.* 3.39.3–16.

22. See R. Bauckham, *Jesus and the Eyewitnesses* (Grand Rapids: Eerdmans, 2006), pp. 417–420.

23. Papias mistakenly calls him 'Philip the apostle' (Eusebius, *Hist. eccl.* 3.39.9).

It will be helpful to set out the chain of tradition implied by Papias's comments in an earlier passage (see fig. 12.2 below).

29–33	80	120
The Lord		

      What the disciples of the Lord *said*

      [Andrew, Peter, Philip, Thomas, James, John, Matthew]

                              What Aristion and John the Elder *say*

                                                Papias writes

Fig. 12.2 Jesus to Papias.

Overlapping transmission is implied. Papias heard what John the Elder *was saying* (*c.* 120); John the Elder *heard* what the disciples of the Lord *said* (*c.* 80); disciples of the Lord [*heard* the Lord] (*c.* 29–33). Papias heard the 'living and abiding' voice of the disciples of the Lord through their hearer, the Elder. Papias does not have to depend on unprofitable 'things out of books' but on the witness of the disciples of the Lord mediated through Aristion and the Elder. The chain of transmission is short – less than a century. Moreover, and of great importance, according to the Elder, Mark's wellspring of information for his Gospel was Peter, the leading disciple and apostle of the Lord.

Justin Martyr

We cannot overestimate the importance of this great teacher and writer, for two reasons. To begin with, Justin's extensive details of his theology and activities probably reveal church practice and beliefs that had been in place in the previous decades, if only we had the sources to inform us.

At the same time, Justin's writings are the crucial link in the chain that within a few decades connected to Irenaeus, who wrote of the *quadriform* (fourfold) Gospel (Matthew, Mark, Luke, John), and to Tatian, who wove the four Gospels into one combined Gospel, the *Diatessaron* (which means '[one] through four').

In *c.* 150 Justin Martyr provides the earliest glimpse into the extent of activities typically occurring in the house-church meeting, not only in Rome but also universally within the empire. He writes, 'On the day called Sunday, *all who live in the cities or in the country* gather together in one place . . . '[24] Justin means his reader (the emperor Antoninus Pius) to understand he is speaking about church practices *everywhere.*

In his *1 Apology* 65–67 Justin gives extensive detail about a typical church meeting.[25] After a *baptism* 'where there is water' the baptized is brought to 'the place where the other Christians are assembled' and where they pray for the newly baptized. This was followed by the members' *kiss* of mutual greeting. Then the lector *read* at length from the *memoirs of the apostles* (the Gospels) or the writings of the prophets, upon which the president 'instructs and exhorts' the people, based on these readings.[26]

Marcion

Marcion of Sinope came to Rome *c.* 144, though there is debate whether his idiosyncratic views were formulated there or beforehand.[27] Marcion appears to have been both a Gnostic and a radical Paulinist who rejected the Jewish God and the Jewish Law. In his major work *Antitheses* Marcion limited his recognition of New Testament writings to those that de-emphasized Christianity's Jewish roots as much as possible. Accordingly Marcion accepted only an

---

24. *Ante-Nicene Fathers: The Writings of the Fathers down to A. D. 325*, ed. A. Roberts and J. Donaldson, rev. A. C. Coxe (New York: Christian Literature, 1885), *1 Apol.* 67, italics added.

25. Ibid. 65–67.

26. See 1 Tim. 4:13, 'Until I come devote yourself to the *reading*, the *exhortation* and the *teaching*' (my tr.).

27. Marcion's teachings are known only through those who refuted him, chiefly Justin Martyr, Irenaeus, Tertullian and Hippolytus. According to R. L. Fox, *Pagans and Christians* (New York: Knopf, 1989), p. 516, Marcion's views were sufficiently well known to have been used by Celsus in his attack on Christianity.

expurgated version of Luke's Gospel[28] and of Paul's letters.[29] The point is that Marcion's canon points to the currency of the Gospel of Luke.

Summary

Papias's words from the first decades of the second century indicate his dependence on the 'living voice' that went back to the original disciples to inform him about the origin of the Gospels of Mark and Matthew. In passing, Papias refers indirectly also to the Gospels of Luke and John. In the middle of the century Justin describes the universal and well-established practice of the reading of the 'memoirs of the apostles'. Marcion's 'canon' points to the existence and currency of the Gospel of Luke.

Early references from the Gospels

The writers who follow the apostles make extensive reference to the New Testament, though these are frequently imprecise allusions or echoes. These were the early days of Christianity and it would be unreasonable to expect the accomplished and precise scholarship that developed in the following centuries.

Clement of Rome

In *c.* 95 Clement, a leader of the Christians in Rome, wrote a letter to the church in Corinth appealing to them to stop their factionalism

---

28. Marcion omitted from Luke (1) the 'Jewish' chapters 1 and 2, (2) temptation narrative in 4:3 (referring to Deuteronomy), (3) Jesus' claim – while teaching in a synagogue – that his ministry was a fulfilment of the OT (4:16–30), (4) reference to 'the old is good' (5:39), and (5) reference to Jesus' family (8:19).

29. Marcion eliminated from Paul's letters (1) Abraham as an example of faith (Gal. 3:6–9), (2) the connection between the law and the Gospels (Gal. 3:15–25), (3) Rom. 1:19 – 21:1; 3:21 – 4:25, and most of Rom. 9 – 11, and everything after Rom. 14:23. See further F. F. Bruce, *The Canon of Scripture* (Glasgow: Chapter House, 1988), p. 140.

and become a united congregation. Clement weaves many allusions from the New Testament into his letter, including these examples from the Gospels:

> For He said this: '*Show mercy, that you may receive mercy; forgive, that you may be forgiven. As you do, so shall it be done to you. As you give, so shall it be given to you. As you judge, so shall you be judged. As you show kindness, so shall kindness be shown to you. With the measure you use, it will be measured to you.*' (1 Clem. 13.2; cf. Matt. 5:7; 6:14; Luke 6:31, 36–38)

> for he said: '*Woe to that man! It would have been good for him if he had not been born, than that he should cause one of my elect to sin. It would have been better for him to have been tied to a millstone and cast into the sea, than that he should pervert* one of my elect.' (1 Clem. 46.8; cf. Matt. 26:24; Luke 17:1–2)

> '*The sower went forth*', and cast into the earth each of the seeds. (1 Clem. 24.5; cf. Mark 4:3)

The words are close to the passages in the Gospels of Matthew and Luke, but not identical with them. It seems that Clement is loosely quoting and adapting these Gospel texts for the pastoral circumstances of the Corinthians.

This is consistent with his 'free' use of passages from the Acts of the Apostles and the letters in the New Testament.

> Moreover, you were all humble and free from arrogance, submitting rather than demanding submission, '*more glad to give than to receive . . .* ' (1 Clem. 2.1; cf. Acts 20:35)

> But of his Son the Master spoke thus: '*You are my Son; today I have begotten you.* Ask of me, and I will give you the Gentiles for your inheritance, and the ends of the earth for your possession.' And again he says to him: 'Sit at my right hand, until I make your enemies a footstool for your feet.' (1 Clem. 36.4–5; cf. Heb. 1:5)

Every faction and every schism was abominable to you. You mourned
for the transgressions of your neighbours: you considered their
shortcomings to be your own. You never once regretted doing good,
but were *'ready for every good work'*. (1 Clem. 2.6–7; cf. Titus 3:1)

Love unites us with God; *'love covers a multitude of sins'*; *love endures all things,
is patient in all things* ... (1 Clem. 49.5; cf. 1 Pet. 4:8; 1 Cor. 13:7)[30]

We note as a matter of importance that Clement makes pastoral use
of Matthew, Luke, the book of Acts, 1 Corinthians, Titus and
1 Peter. Clearly this establishes that these New Testament texts were
in circulation and use by the time Clement wrote in AD 95.

Ignatius

Ignatius, Bishop of Antioch, wrote seven letters in the course of
his journey to Rome, where he was to be executed. The dating is
uncertain, between 110 and 117. We find echoes of three of the
Gospels in Ignatius' letters: Matthew, Luke and John.

No one professing faith sins, nor does anyone possessing love hate.
'The tree is known by its fruit'; thus those who profess to be Christ's will be
recognized by their actions. For the work is not a matter of what one
promises now, but of persevering to the end in the power of faith.
(*Eph.* 14.2; cf. Matt. 12:33)

and when he came to Peter and those with him, he said to them:
'Take hold of me; handle me and see that I am not a disembodied demon.' And
immediately they touched him and believed, being closely united with his
flesh and blood. For this reason they too despised death; indeed, they
proved to be greater than death. And after his resurrection he ate and
drank with them like one who is composed of flesh, although spiritually
he was united with the Father. (*Smyrn.* 3.2–3; cf. Luke 24:39)

---

30. M. W. Holmes (ed.), *The Apostolic Fathers: Greek Texts and Translations*
(Grand Rapids: Baker, 1992).

For even though certain people wanted to deceive me, humanly speaking, nevertheless *the Spirit* is not deceived, because it is from God; for it *knows from where it comes and where it is going*, and exposes the hidden things. (*Philadelph.* 7.1; cf. John 3:8)[31]

Ignatius also makes extensive use of passages from the letters of the New Testament, which he freely adapts:

I pray that you will listen to me in love, so that I won't, by virtue of having written to you, be a witness against you. But also pray for me, for I need your love in the mercy of God so that I may be reckoned worthy of the fate which I am eager to obtain, in order that *I not be found disqualified.* (*Trall.* 12.3; cf. 1 Cor. 9:27)

Do not be misled, my brothers: those who adulterously corrupt households '*will not inherit the kingdom of God*'. (*Eph.* 16.1; cf. 1 Cor. 6:9–10)

From Syria all the way to Rome I am fighting with wild beasts, on land and sea, by night and day, chained amidst ten leopards (that is, a company of soldiers) who only get worse when they are well-treated. Yet because of their mistreatment I am becoming more of a disciple; nevertheless '*I am not thereby justified.*' (*Rom.* 5.1; cf. 1 Cor. 4:4)[32]

These citations are not comprehensive but are given to illustrate Ignatius' familiarity with and adaptation of passages from three of the Gospels and various letters of the New Testament, including Romans, 1 Corinthians and Ephesians.

Polycarp
Polycarp, Bishop of Smyrna and a disciple of the apostle John, wrote his letter to the Philippians soon after the death of Ignatius

31. Ibid.
32. Ibid.

(*Phil.* 1.1; 9.1; 13.1), that is, *c.* 120. Polycarp's letter is punctuated by numerous quotations from and allusions to New Testament texts. As in the following two examples Polycarp quotes from the Gospels of Matthew and Luke:

> but instead remembering what the Lord said as he taught: '*Do not judge, that you may not be judged; forgive, and you will be forgiven; show mercy, that you may be shown mercy; with the measure you use, it will be measured back to you*'; and, '*blessed are the poor and those who are persecuted for righteousness' sake, for theirs is the kingdom of God*'. (*Phil.* 2.3; cf. Matt. 7:1–2; Luke 6:36–38; 6:20)

> Therefore let us leave behind the worthless speculation of the crowd and let us return to the word delivered to us from the beginning; let us be self-controlled with respect to prayer and persevere in fasting, earnestly asking the all-seeing God '*to lead us not into temptation*' because, as the Lord said, '*the spirit is indeed willing, but the flesh is weak*'. (*Phil.* 7.2; cf. Matt. 6:13; 26:41)[33]

Polycarp also quotes from or alludes to the book of Acts and to the majority of the letters of the New Testament, including Romans, 1 and 2 Corinthians, Galatians, Ephesians, Philippians, 1 and 2 Timothy, Hebrews, 1 Peter and 1 John. In contrast with Clement and Ignatius we find that Polycarp includes a greater concentration of New Testament texts and he does so with more precise quotation of those texts. One of many examples illustrates this:

> '*Though you have not seen him, you believe in him with an inexpressible and glorious joy*' (which many desire to experience), knowing that '*by grace you have been saved, not because of works*' but by the will of God through Jesus Christ. (*Phil.* 1.3; cf. 1 Pet. 1:8; Eph. 2:5)[34]

---

33. Ibid.
34. Ibid.

Summary

The letters of Clement (*c.* 95), Ignatius and Polycarp (*c.* 120) follow immediately the era of the apostles. Clement and Ignatius freely adapt New Testament texts but, because he was a more careful scholar, Polycarp tends to quote those texts more precisely. Taken together we are able to say that these writers are familiar with at least three of the Gospels and the great majority of the letters of the New Testament. Missing from these writers is any clear reference to the book of Revelation, though it would be precarious to speculate its non-existence.

The geographical spread of these sources is highly significant. Clement writes from Rome, Ignatius had been based in Antioch in Syria, and Polycarp writes from Smyrna in Roman Asia. The letters of these men point to the earliness of the texts of the New Testament that they quote, but also importantly their wide geographical extent.

Early manuscripts of the Gospels

We are very fortunate that many portions of early Gospel manuscripts have survived the ravages of time.[35] The fragments in table 12.6 opposite have been found in Egypt (where there is minimal humidity). We know that they were originally written in codex (early book) form since there is writing on the front and back of the leaves.

The chance survival of fragile papyri in the sands of Egypt is evidence that John, Matthew and Luke were in circulation and use by the first quarter of the second century, and that all four canonical Gospels were in circulation and use by the end of the second century.

These fragments were originally part of codexes read in church meetings from the end of the apostolic age. Conspicuously absent is any surviving fragment of the Gospel of Mark. Yet Matthew's

---

35. See P. W. Comfort, *The Quest for the Original Texts of the New Testament* (Grand Rapids: Baker, 1992), pp. 31–32.

Table 12.6 Papyrus manuscripts of the second century

Papyrus	Date	Content
P^{52}	Early 2nd C.	A few verses of John 18
P^{67}	c. 125–150	A few verses from Matt. 3, 5
P^{64}	c. 125–150	A few verses from Matt. 26
P^{4}	c. 125–150	Portions of Luke 1 – 4
P^{75}	c. 175	Portions of Luke 3 – 7, 9, 17, 22
		Much of John
P^{77}	c. 175–200	A few verses of Matt. 23
P^{103}	c. 175–200	A few verses from Matt. 13 – 14
P^{104}	c. 175–200	A few verses from Matt. 21
P^{90}	c. 175–200	A portion of John 18 – 19
P^{1}	c. 200	Portions of Matt. 1
P^{66}	c. 200	Most of John
P^{45}	c. 200	Portions of all four Gospels and Acts

and Luke's reproduction of Mark in the body of their Gospels, as agreed by most scholars, establishes the prior existence of Mark. While most surviving fragments of John come from the late second century, the discovery of P^{52}, dating from the first half of the second century, establishes a first-century origin of this Gospel. Furthermore, the extensive parts of John in P^{90}, P^{75}, P^{66} and P^{45} support the widespread early use of this Gospel.

Summary
The three strands of evidence – early references *to* the Gospels, early quotations and allusions *from* the Gospels, and surviving manuscript copies *of* the Gospels – when considered together are compelling evidence that the four canonical Gospels and the major letters of the New Testament were in circulation and use by the end of the first century, that is, the century of Jesus.

Recovering the text of the New Testament[36]

Due to the rapid spread of early Christianity and the need of copies of texts for reading in the churches a vast number of manuscripts of the New Testament have survived from the early centuries. Following Constantine's adoption of Christianity, the proliferation of copied texts increased.

To date there are more than 5,600 copies of part or whole Greek New Testament manuscripts and more than 19,000 copies that were translated into Latin, Syriac, Armenian or Coptic 'versions' from the original Greek. Due to the ravages of weather and persecution these 24,000 surviving texts represent a mere fraction of the original numbers of manuscripts. Furthermore the rather verbose Church Fathers from the early centuries quoted at such length from the apostolic writings that it is almost possible to recover the New Testament from their 'citations' of its texts alone.

By contrast, we have only a small number of manuscripts for 'classical' authors from the era of the New Testament. For example, there are fifteen manuscripts of Josephus' *Jewish Antiquities*, the earliest of which is from the ninth century. There are twenty manuscripts of Tacitus' *Annals of Imperial Rome*, the earliest of which is from the ninth century; but of his original sixteen books, Books 7–10 are missing, and Books 5, 6, 11 and 16 are incomplete. It is generally the same for manuscripts of other authors from classical antiquity; for example, we have eight copies of Suetonius (from the tenth century) and seven copies of Pliny the Younger (from the eighth century). For the recovery of the words of the original texts historians of classical antiquity have only a tiny fraction of the manuscripts available to textual critics of the New Testament.

---

36. See generally P. D. Wegner, *Textual Criticism of the Bible* (Downers Grove: InterVarsity Press, 2006). For the 'dialogue' between Bart Ehrman and Daniel Wallace see R. B. Stewart, B. D. Ehrman (contributor) and D. B. Wallace (contributor), *Bart D. Ehrman and Daniel B. Wallace in Dialogue: The Reliability of the New Testament* (Minneapolis: Fortress, 2011).

Sceptics point to the abundance of copyists' errors in New Testament manuscripts. These errors were due to poor levels of literacy (many scribes were amateurs) and to intentional 'improvements' of the copied texts. Yet these errors should be regarded as positives, in two ways. First, they demonstrate an absence of collusion, thus dispelling conspiracy theories about the origin of the New Testament. Secondly, the patterns of errors have allowed textual critics over several centuries to group the thousands of texts and 'citations' broadly into four main geographic 'families' that share common traditions of agreements and divergences.

The four main 'families' are the *Alexandrian* (B text), the *Caesarean* (the C text), the *Western* (D text) and the *Byzantine* (the A text). Within these 'families' – to generalize – we have (1) Greek texts, (2) translated 'versions', and (3) 'citations' from the church fathers.

By painstaking cross-checking and the development of practical guidelines (e.g. 'take the harder reading'; 'take the shorter reading') textual critics are able to reconstruct a text of the New Testament that according to some estimates is 99% accurate in relationship to the original autographs of the original writers. Furthermore it is claimed that no point of Christian doctrine depends on the 'variant' readings between the manuscripts.

Examples of problematic texts include the longer version of Mark (verses 9–20) and the woman taken in adultery (John 8:53 – 9:11). Apart from these longer passages most variants relate to single words or phrases, for example, *'we have* peace with God' or *'let us have* peace with God' (Rom. 5:1). Modern translations like the English Standard Version (ESV) note these variants as footnotes and they occur on average at the rate of about one per page.

The principles of textual criticism as applied to the New Testament are the same as for other ancient texts, for example, Josephus' *Jewish Antiquities*. Employing the same methods as those who edit and publish texts for the Greek New Testament, scholars group the surviving texts into 'families' and seek to recover the most likely text.

Conclusion

We are able to establish the events and phases in early Christianity with relative certainty.

Jesus (28–33)
  (a) Oral and written traditions (33–65)
  (b) Gospels (65–80)
  (c) Post-apostolic era (95–130)

The impact of Jesus was very great, the evidence for which is the missionary movement he established, as reflected in the body of mission literature, the New Testament. Moving backwards from *c* the post-apostolic period confirms *b*, the existence of the Gospels and the major letters; moving backwards from *b*, the Gospels confirm the existence of *a*, the mission of the apostles and their oral and written traditions; moving backwards from *a*, the oral and written traditions bear witness to *Jesus himself, and his resurrection from the dead.* Such a reconstruction is credible and makes sense historically. The chronological identification of phases and events inexorably and relentlessly points in just one direction: to the astonishing impact of Jesus the Christ, risen from the dead.

It must be insisted that the line of argument above is historical, not theological. The basis of the argument is one of cause and effect. The 'effects' are successive bodies of mission literature attributable to just one 'cause', the impact of the historical figure of Jesus. By analogy, the existence of the community at Qumran and the literature of the Dead Sea Scrolls prompt the question 'Who or what was the impetus for these "effects"?' The answer is, the Teacher of Righteousness, the founder of the community at Qumran.

The analogy, however, is not strong, because the Teacher of Righteousness is a shadowy figure and his relationship with the Qumran community and the Scrolls is debatable. The case of Jesus, by contrast, is strong and direct. Jesus impacted his disciples, who prepared oral and written teachings that soon assumed written form in the Gospels that soon began to be referred to and quoted and whose very early copies go back to the early part of the second century.

In short, the case for the integrity of the early traditions and the copying and transmission of the texts is very strong indeed.

13. GOSPEL TRUTH AND REVELATION

the mystery of Christ . . . was not made known to the sons of men in other generations as it has now been revealed to his holy apostles and prophets by the Spirit.

Ephesians 3:4–5

Believing scientists such as Lennox and Collins effectively argue for the existence of the Intelligent Mind who has created the universe and has created intelligent minds in humans, who are able to comprehend the grandeur and intricacy of the universe and of life within the universe.

The New Atheists pour scorn on any modern person who believes in God and the miracles of Jesus. But thanks to the efforts of Lennox, Collins and others we are able with good conscience and without embarrassment to accept the credibility of the Creator *and* the miracles of Jesus.

These scientists readily agree that whilst physics, genetics and biology point to the reality of God, they are unable to *identify* God for us so we can know him. It is at this point that the issue of gospel truth becomes critical. It is in and through the gospel that the otherwise unknown 'God' shows his face.

The New Atheists understand this, which explains why they have launched their sustained attacks on the 'truth' of the gospel. Destroy that 'truth', they believe, and you destroy the gospel, and its fallacious claims to 'reveal' the identity of God.

This book has defended gospel truth. Its method has been to appeal to history-based argument. It began by standing back and taking in the wide angle of faith statements by Ignatius in his letters (written some time between AD 110 and 117) and Paul in AD 48. In AD 48, a mere fifteen years after Jesus, Paul declared that Jesus is the Son of God, and seventy years later Ignatius too stated that Jesus is the Son of God. We conclude that from very early times Jesus was held to be the Son of God and that, therefore, Ignatius did not inflate Jesus, a mere man, into a divine figure. From the beginning of Christian history Jesus was regarded as the Son of God. This is historical fact.

Christopher Hitchens did not think Jesus ever existed, although few other New Atheists adopt such an extreme viewpoint. Based on the secular sources Josephus, Tacitus and Pliny we can say with confidence that Jesus (who was called 'Christ') was executed by the Romans in Judea during the prefecture of Pilate (AD 26–36), and that the movement quickly spread throughout the empire, including to Rome and Bithynia. Historians of all persuasions believe Jesus was a true figure of history.

The New Atheists claim that world history contradicts historical statements in the New Testament, including, as outlined in chapter 5, the details of the birth of Jesus during the census conducted by Quirinius (Luke 2:2). In response it was noted that in Luke-Acts, which covers seventy years, we find sixteen 'linkages' from that narrative into world history. It was pointed out that such a large number of confirmed connections are impressive, even if the census reference remains a problem. Luke's apparent error may be due to his awkward grammar or, less probably, to the source material he depended on in good faith. In any case, Luke's reference to 'the *first* census' implies a sequence of later censuses. There is no record of later censuses in Palestine, however, thus leaving open the possibility of an earlier census, especially since the adjective 'first' can mean 'former' (as in Acts 1:1, 'the first [i.e. former] book'). In the light of Luke's overall competence displayed throughout Luke-Acts many fair-minded historians are prepared to give Luke the benefit of the doubt regarding the census of Quirinius.

Archaeological discoveries have cumulatively confirmed the historicity of the New Testament narrative, from Bethlehem to Patmos. Some discoveries are 'general', for example, the *insulae* (apartments) in Capernaum or the ancient boat found in the lake. Others are more specific, such as the inscription bearing the name Pontius Pilate (in Caesarea Maritima), the ossuary engraved with the name Joseph Caiaphas (in Jerusalem) or the inscription with the names of the Paulii family (in Antioch in Pisidia). Together, these discoveries – frequently 'accidental' in the course of building excavations, for example – undergird the historical spine that runs through the entire New Testament.

One of the New Atheists' main lines of attack is the 'contradictions' between the Gospels. In particular they seize on differences between the nativity stories in Matthew and Luke and between John and the other three Gospels. Here they display little understanding of the nature of biography writing or history writing in the Greco-Roman world of that era and the limitations under which their authors laboured. When the gospel writers are measured against their 'secular' contemporaries, they prove to be careful with the facts and reliable in what they write.

The New Atheists fail to understand that the Gospels, as we have them, are the final 'written-up' versions of oral and written mission traditions that had been created for church use in the several decades between Jesus and the writing of the Gospels. That there are *four* Gospels indicates that their authors were providing texts for church reading for audiences of different ethnicity and geographical location. Inevitably they 'bring out' different emphases for differing readerships. Indeed if they were slavishly identical we would suspect collusion. Their divergences in detail and emphasis point to their independence and to the underlying historicity of what they write.

Matthew and Luke, despite their differing birth narratives, including irreconcilable genealogies, agree about the core facts. Jesus was conceived by supernatural intervention in Mary, who was betrothed to Joseph, and the child was born in Bethlehem in the days of Herod the king, and raised in Nazareth. The accounts are clearly independent, yet bear witness to an underlying historicity.

Mark and John make quite different emphases in their Gospels, but agree about the global narrative that Jesus exercised his ministry in Galilee in the presence of twelve disciples before journeying to Jerusalem, where he was arrested, put on trial before Jewish leaders and the Roman governor, who ordered his execution. This broad agreement is the more impressive because Mark and John wrote their Gospels independently of each other. Although more symbolically reflective, John's Gospel is deeply rooted in the topography and architecture of Jerusalem within a historical setting in Judea when Pilate was governor of the province and Annas and Caiaphas were the incumbent high priests in Jerusalem.

The New Atheists mock anyone in modern times who believes in the miracles of Jesus. Their commitment to the proposition that there is 'no God' locks them into a 'closed' universe in which the regularities of life absolutely preclude the possibility of a miracle, which by their definition is necessarily unobserved. Lennox makes the important distinction between the 'uniformity of nature' (based on observation – Hume's argument) and '*absolute* uniformity' (based on a singular event that had not been observed). By way of example, the 'Big Bang' by which the universe began was a singular, unrepeatable and unobserved event contrary to our experience. The New Atheists' presuppositions that the irregular cannot occur would rule out the possibility of the 'Big Bang'.

When the canons of history are applied to the miracles of Jesus – in particular their sheer frequency and multiple, independent attestation – we reasonably conclude that these events actually happened. From a historian's point of view that is an entirely reasonable assertion, based on evidence.

The Gospels speak of miracles *by* Jesus and miracles where Jesus was the *object* of God's action. The virginal conception marked Jesus' entry into mundane history, and his resurrection from the dead was the sure sign that God had vindicated his Son against the human and cosmic forces that combined to bring about his death. As with his miracles, the evidence from the frequency of his resurrection 'appearances' and their multiple, independent attestation speaks powerfully for the historical truth of Jesus' resurrection from the dead.

The New Atheists claim that 'gospels' from later centuries have the same basis for acceptance as the Gospels in our Bibles. This is a strange argument since they think the biblical Gospels are useless anyway! Furthermore they contend that the tradition between Jesus and the Gospels is so deeply flawed, and those Gospels so miscopied subsequently, that there is no way we can confidently know about the historical Jesus.

This is yet another realm of knowledge where the New Atheists are uninformed. They happily seize the opinions of a few sceptics in this field, whereas the majority of textual critics are confident that the reconstructed texts of our Gospels are close to the texts as originally written by Matthew, Mark, Luke and John. The early references *to* the Gospels, the early quotations and echoes *from* the Gospels, and the discovery of early manuscripts *of* the Gospels combine to point to integrity of those texts, as reconstructed, printed in our Bibles.

In sum, the history-based attacks by the New Atheists when examined prove to be unsustainable. Overwhelmingly the texts of the New Testament can survive rigorous and honest scrutiny, as I trust the arguments in this book have shown.

There is a great gulf, however, between accepting responses to these attacks and subscribing to Christian belief. Many people agree intellectually about the truth question but shrug their shoulders and say the Christian faith is not for them.

This reality powerfully reminds us that historical arguments, like the scientific ones employed by Lennox and Collins, take us only so far. Of themselves these arguments, honest and good as they are, do not touch the inner wellsprings of the human heart. Something else is needed.

Revelation

'Revelation' is one of the key words in the New Testament. Its everyday meaning was to 'uncover' something that was covered, like the contents of a pot with a lid on. 'To reveal' metaphorically meant 'to open the eyes' to something in front of you that you did not really understand. Jesus spoke parables to the multitudes that they did not comprehend, although they were couched in simple, homely terms. Turning to the disciples in private he said, 'To you *has been given* the secret of the kingdom of God', whereupon he explained the meaning of the parable that had been opaque to the multitudes and to them (Mark 4:11). Later he stated that the truth of his identity was 'hidden' from the 'wise and understanding' but that he, Jesus, was *'revealing'* this truth to 'babes' like the disciples (Matt. 11:25–27). When at last Peter publicly declared Jesus to be the Christ, he was told that 'flesh and blood' had not *revealed* it to him, but the Father in heaven had (Matt. 16:17).

What is the relationship between historical truth – the subject of this book – and *revealed* gospel truth? Historical truth is fundamental. Would anyone bother thinking about Jesus if he or she regarded the New Testament to be full of errors? Some people simply accept the Bible because it *is* the Bible, whilst others come to accept it because of arguments like those in this book. Either way, the Gospels must be seen as historically credible before one takes the further step of an inner commitment to their message.

That further step requires openness and humility before God. As Jesus said, he reveals himself to 'babes' but not to the 'wise and understanding'.

God's chosen way of revealing himself to us is by means of the gospel (the good news), that is, the written gospel or the spoken gospel that is true to the written gospel. Paul stated that it was 'in' the gospel that God *reveals* his righteousness, that is, his saving love to those alienated from God because of their rebellion (Rom. 1:17).

At the conclusion of Romans Paul offers this moving doxology to God:

> Now to him who is able to strengthen you according to my gospel and
> the preaching of Jesus Christ, according to the *revelation* of the mystery
> that was kept secret for long ages but has now been disclosed and
> through the prophetic writings has been made known to all nations,
> according to the command of the eternal God, to bring about the
> obedience of faith – to the only wise God be glory for evermore
> through Jesus Christ! Amen. (Rom. 16:25–27)

From these tightly packed words we learn that through the 'gospel', that is, the 'preaching of Jesus Christ', God has *revealed* (unveiled) the mystery that was long hidden in the prophetic writings of the Old Testament. Through this gospel about Jesus Christ, who fulfils the prophetic writings, God brings about the 'obedience of faith'.

There are two elements that work together. One is the *statement* of the gospel centred on Christ's fulfilling the messianic prophecies of the Old Testament. The other is the obedient *response of faith* (in Christ) to that gospel message.

We notice that Paul says nothing about the issue of historical reliability, of gospel truth, but we can be sure he assumes that truth as a precondition to the exercise of faith in Christ as based on the gospel message about Christ.

There is an organic connection between Jesus, the oral and written traditions his disciples created and the texts of the letters and Gospels that comprise the New Testament. They are the 'Scriptures' of the gospel, the gospel that is the message about Jesus Christ. These texts of the New Testament are the completed 'deposit' of the gospel, the 'word' about and from Jesus Christ. This is why the early Christians treasured these texts and read them to one another in their churches.

The reading of the Scriptures

The passage from Romans 16:25 refers to both the prophetic writings *and* the preaching of Jesus Christ. This neatly symbolizes the two testaments in our Bibles and helps us understand how from early times our Christian forefathers provided for the public reading in churches of the Old and New Testaments.

Reading in the synagogues

It is evident that the core activity in the synagogues in the time of Jesus was the public reading of the Holy Scriptures, as two examples indicate. The first is Theodotus' synagogue in Jerusalem for Jews of the Diaspora that was dedicated to 'the *reading* of the law and the *teaching* of the commandments'.[1] The second relates to Jesus, who entered the synagogue in Nazareth and was handed the scroll of Isaiah, from which he *read* and then taught that the prophet's words were fulfilled in him (Luke 4:16–17).

These examples point to the fact that for Jews *canonically* recognized texts (the Law and the Prophets) only were *publicly read* in the synagogues.[2] Jewish scribes wrote paraphrases of texts and commentaries on texts but, so far as we know, these were not read publicly in the synagogues. Public reading of a text was the sign of the divine authority of the text.

Reading in the churches

It is highly significant, therefore, that the first Christians (who were Jews) *publicly read* their texts in their meetings, conferring on them the same status Jews had ascribed to the Law, the Prophets and the Writings. Following are some examples of the public reading of New Testament texts.

---

1. R. Riesner, 'Synagogues in Jerusalem', in R. Bauckham (ed.), *The Book of Acts in Its First Century Setting* (Grand Rapids: Eerdmans, 1995), vol. 4, pp. 192–200, italics added.

2. E. E. Ellis, *The Making of the New Testament Documents* (Leiden: Brill, 2002), p. 353, n. 62, noted that, 'In Judaism only canonical scripture could be *read* in the synagogue. Even the Aramaic targum, i.e. paraphrastic translation of Scripture, had to be rendered *orally*' – italics original.

A Gospel

> But when you see the abomination of desolation standing where it ought
> not to be (let the *reader* [lector] understand), then let those who are in
> Judea flee to the mountains. (Mark 13:14)

Mark is directing the public reader (the lector) of his text to 'understand' what Jesus meant by 'the abomination of desolation standing
where "he" or "it" ought not to be' (i.e. in the temple). Mark's
direction implies that the reader will explain the meaning of these
words to those who are *hearing* them.

Letters of Paul

> And when this letter has been *read* among you, have it also *read* in the
> church of the Laodiceans; and see that you also *read* the letter from
> Laodicea. (Col. 4:16)

Paul is expecting his letters to be copied, exchanged and *read* in the
churches.

Reading as the work of a minister

> Until I come, devote yourself to the [public] *reading* of Scripture, to
> *exhortation*, to *teaching*. (1 Tim. 4:13)

> Blessed is the one who *reads* aloud the words of this prophecy, and
> blessed are those who *hear*, and who *keep* what is written in it, for the
> time is near. (Rev. 1:3)

These words come from Paul and John to their respective *public*
readers in churches. Paul directed Timothy, a minister, to *read*
(publicly) Scripture, and to preach and teach thereon. By 'Scripture'
Paul meant the Old Testament, but New Testament writings also,
including Paul's own letters.

John is pronouncing a blessing on the public readers of his book
of Revelation within the seven congregations in Roman Asia to
which it was sent. It is possible that the *public reader* was the 'angel'
in the churches John was addressing (e.g. Rev. 2:1). John also
pronounces his blessing upon those who *hear* and *keep* what they
have heard.

These passages indicate that three different genres of text (gospel,
letter, apocalyptic) were read (aloud) in church. Just as in the synagogues the public reading of texts indicated that they were regarded
as 'canonical', as the oracles of God.

Reading from the Old and New Testaments in the second century

Justin Martyr was a church leader in Rome. In *c.* 150 he describes
a typical church meeting at that time: 'On the day called Sunday
. . . the memoirs of the apostles [which are called Gospels] or
the writings of the prophets are *read* as long as time permits . . . '
(*1 Apol.* 66–67).[3]

This is an early example of the reading of both the Old and New
Testament in the churches. Jesus read from the Old Testament and
declared its promises fulfilled in him (Luke 4:16–21; 24:44–47).
Likewise Paul stated that the promises of God found an eternal 'yes'
in Jesus Christ, the Son of God, whom he, Silvanus and Timothy
preached to the Corinthians (2 Cor. 1:20). Justin's information tells
us that the early Christians read both Old and New Testament
passages, implying that both enjoyed a canonical status in the
churches.

Confirmation of Justin's words is to be found in the nature of
the New Testament manuscripts from the second century. Without
exception these surviving pieces of papyri are written on both sides,
indicating, as we have seen, that they were originally part of codexes
and not scrolls. Almost certainly the Christians of that era wrote

---

3. A. C. Coxe, *The Ante Nicene Fathers*, vol. 1: *The Apostolic Fathers with Justin Martyr and Irenaeus* (Grand Rapids: Eerdmans, 1884).

their copies of the New Testament in book form to facilitate reading and teaching in churches.

Summary and reflection

The public reading of the texts of the New Testament is evidence that the early Christians treated them as 'Scripture' in extension and fulfilment of the Sacred Writings of the Old Testament. Accordingly they regarded them as 'God-breathed' and authoritative for faith and life (2 Tim. 3:16–17). The Gospel of John is especially important since its author tells us of Jesus' promise to send the 'Spirit of truth', who would 'guide' the disciples 'into all the truth' (John 16:13–14). Various passages in this Gospel help us understand the processes by which the Spirit 'guided' the original disciples into the truth that was subsequently written in this Gospel (see John 2:22; 7:38; 12:16).

It was the public reading of texts in the churches that conveyed a de facto canonical status on texts. Criteria for a text's canonical status included that it was written by an apostle or an apostle's associate, and that it was written within and not later than the generation of the apostles.

Conclusion

Scientific argument convincingly demonstrates the existence of the Intelligent Mind, the Creator and of intelligent minds in us humans. This argument, however, takes us so far but no further.

Historical argument is able to address most of the challenges of the New Atheists. The historical truth of the New Testament is critically important because without a positive conviction about it no sensible person would stake his or her life on a commitment to Christ, a commitment Christ calls us to make. The argument of this book is that the gospel is true in two senses. It is true both *historically* and *ultimately*, that is, as God's *revelation* of himself, his love and his saving ways. It is through the gospel that God knows us humans, which in turn makes it possible for us to know God.

EPILOGUE

What, then, is gospel truth? The answer is, Jesus.

Jesus revealed and embodied the God our eyes cannot see. He shows us who God is and how we 'know' – relate to – God. Jesus is our teacher and our life's example, the one we look to and from whom we learn. He gave sight to the blind, hearing to the deaf, healing to the diseased and disabled, freedom to the demon-possessed and life to the dead.

From Jesus we understand that wrongdoing primarily emanates from within us individually. As the perfect image of God, Jesus showed up wrongdoing by the way people reacted to him. His resolute behaviour exposed the hypocrisy of the Pharisees, the corruption of the chief priests, the cowardice of the Roman governor and the fickleness of his own disciples. Technology has changed, but human foibles continue to be revealed when we stand alongside Jesus.

Thus Jesus helps us understand why human affairs are the way they are. In so far as they are uplifting, it is because they consciously or unconsciously follow his teaching and example. In so far as they are evil, it is because they are contrary to that teaching and example. Jesus is humanity's paradigm and moral template.

Amazingly, however, Jesus was 'the friend of sinners', as the Pharisees disparagingly called him. Jesus condemned those whose pride blinded them to their hypocrisy, corruption, cowardice and fickleness. But he did not condemn those who knew they were 'sinners', 'lost' from God. To them he was 'the good shepherd' who gave his life for such 'sheep' to restore them, forgiven, to God.

His life was taken from him by a convergence of the evils that he said arose from within, the self-interest of the Annas–Caiaphas dynasty, the self-preservation of Pontius Pilate and the self-serving duplicity of Judas Iscariot. Yet in a death that he said he 'must' die was the divinely mandated means for the forgiveness of all who reach out to him in personal trust.

His victory over death is the great 'sign' of hope for humanity caught in the death cycle. That resurrection showed that the evil that killed him did not have the last word, but that God's goodness and truth did and does.

History continues, but with the same human dynamics we see in the Gospels. Those Gospels invite people in every generation to look to Jesus as the great beacon of goodness and hope, but more than that, as the One to believe in and to 'follow'. For that is what a Christian is, a 'follower of Christ'.

There will always be a cost in following him, as he clearly indicated. Those who truly follow him come to replicate the very qualities that expose the same evils in others. The choice to be his follower should not be made lightly.

Those who come to follow him need to do so convinced in mind and conscience that the Gospels are, indeed, historically true. This has been the burden of this small book.

What then does Jesus mean for us who follow him? Above all, he demands the swallowing of pride and the discovery of a humility that will face up to the corruption of our own inner selves. Equally it means the reaching out in trust to the Son of God whom the

Gospels bring before us. Through that act of faith and the sub-sequent life of faith we enter into the God-given freedom from our sense of moral failure and the power of our personal demons. We recommence a journey, now accompanied by the Spirit of Jesus within, in the understanding that his Father is now our Father.

One does not merely drift into becoming a follower of Christ. There has to be a moment of decision and commitment, as there is, for example, in one person's asking and another's accepting commitment to their marriage. By analogy, in that critical moment I will tell God that I have not acknowledged him as I should but have failed to uphold his moral standards; in short, that I am a 'sinner'. In that contrite spirit I will transfer my trust *from* me *to* the One who was crucified and resurrected for me. Like the penitent criminal co-crucified with Jesus, I will say, 'Jesus, remember me when you come in your kingdom.' He will respond, 'Today, you will be with me in Paradise.' That is his promise to all 'sinners' who call out to him. From that time I must be willing to be known as a Christian, including by baptism in his name.

FURTHER READING

Barnett, P. W., *Jesus and the Logic of History* (Leicester: Apollos, 1997)
——, *Messiah, Jesus: The Evidence of History* (Nottingham: Inter-Varsity Press, 2009)
——, *Jesus and the Rise of Early Christianity* (Downers Grove: InterVarsity Press, 1999)
Bauckham, R., *Jesus and the Eyewitnesses* (Grand Rapids: Eerdmans, 2006)
Blomberg, C. L., *The Historical Reliability of the Gospels*, 2nd ed. (Downers Grove: InterVarsity Press; Nottingham: Apollos, 2007)
Hengel, M., *The Four Gospels and the One Gospel of Jesus Christ* (ET London: SCM, 2000)
Wright, N. T., *The Resurrection of the Son of God* (London: SPCK, 2003)

INDEX OF AUTHORS

Fox, R. L., 184n27
Frazer, J., 25–26

Glass, D., 18n7
Gundry, R. H., 175n19

Haenchen, E., 69
Handley, K., 137n3, 146–147
Harris, S., 16, 97, 165
Harvey, J. D., 169n13
Head, P. M., 158
Hemer, C., 69n10, 70–71
Hengel, M., 55, 70–71
Hitchens, C., 16, 17, 22, 32, 35, 42,
    83, 97n2, 97n5, 99, 137, 156, 165,
    166n8
Hoehner, H., 27n4, 64n3, 91n7
Hooper, S., 16n1
Horsley, G. H. R., 79n11

Janssen, L. F., 163n18
Jeremias, J., 115
Judge, E. A., 68

Keener, C., 23n18, 87n3
Kelly, J. N. D., 27n6
Kim, S., 171n15
Koester, H., 158n5

Lake, K., 151n28
Lennox, J., 18n7, 21, 23, 98n6,
    110n2, 112, 113n8, 114, 126

Maier, P., 105n10
Massey, P. T., 84n2

McRay, J., 72n1
Meier, J. P., 119
Meyers, E. M., 116n14
Micklethwait, J., 17n5,
    126n29
Mirecki, P. A., 158n8
Moschos, J., 111n3
Moule, C. F. D., 146
Murphy-O'Connor, J., 80n12

Riesner, R., 27n4, 65n6, 70n11,
    70n13, 77n9, 203n1
Rousseau, J., 72n1, 77n8,
    116n14

Sayer, G., 25n1
Schürer, E., 57n1
Selwyn, E. G., 175n18
Senior, D., 164n21
Sherwin-White, A. N., 68
Skeat, T. C., 157n4, 158n5
Smallwood, E. M., 87n4
Stewart, R. B., 192n36
Strange, J. F., 116n14

Taylor, J. E., 157n3
Tuckett, C., 159–160

Wallace, D. B., 192n36
Wegner, P. D., 192n36
Wells, G. A., 35
Wood, J. H., 160
Wooldridge, A., 17, 126n29
Wright, N. T., 162n16

INDEX OF SCRIPTURE REFRENCES

INDEX OF ANCIENT SOURCES

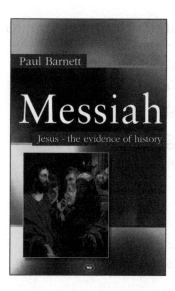

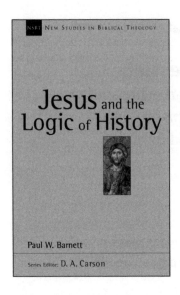